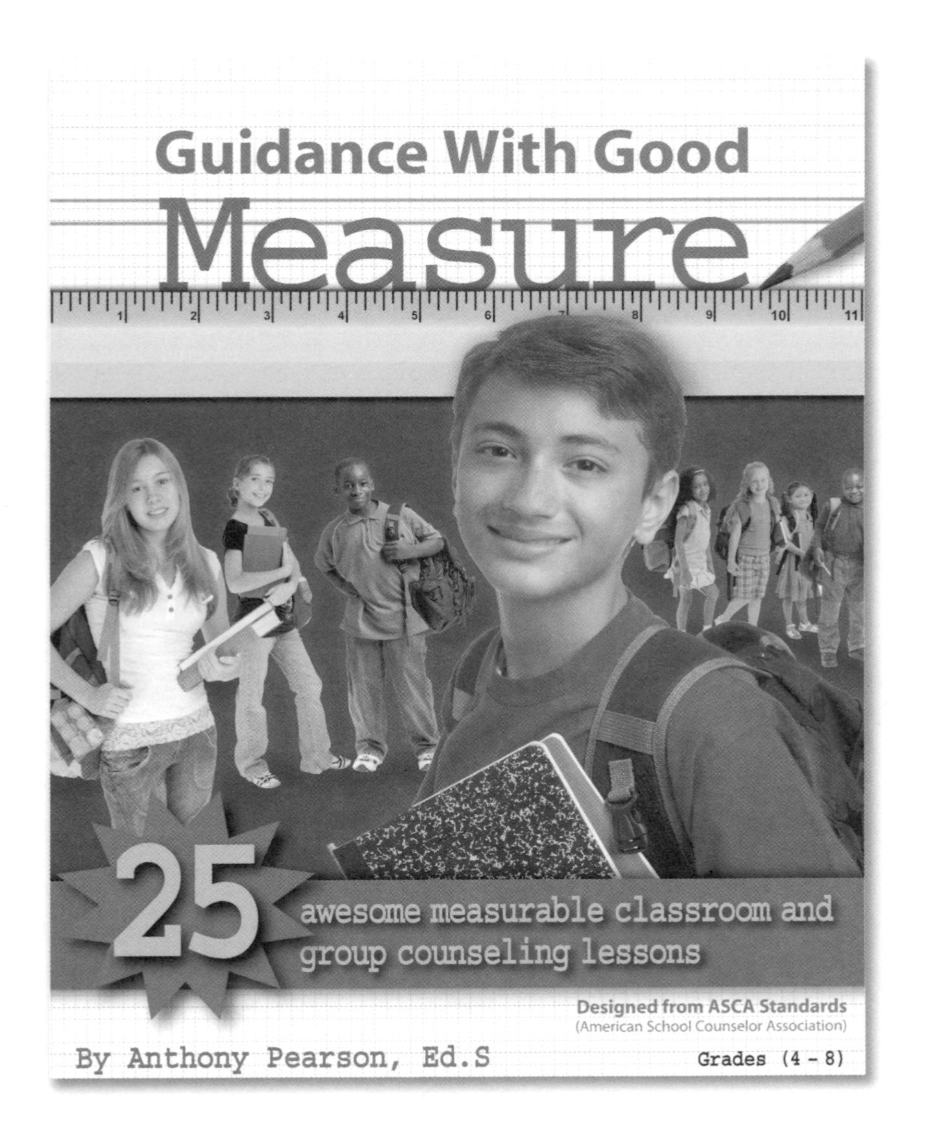
Guidance With Good
Measure
1 2 3 4 5 6 7 8 9 10 11
25
awesome measurable classroom and
group counseling lessons
Designed from ASCA Standards
(American School Counselor Association)
By Anthony Pearson, Ed.S
Grades (4 - 8)

Edited by Susan Bowman

ISBN—978-1-59850-067-7

Library of Congress Control Number:
2008943807

10 9 8 7 6 5 4 3 2 1
Printed in the United States

PO Box 115 • Chapin, SC 29036
(800) 209-9774 • (803) 345-1070 • Fax (803) 345-0888
yl@youthlightbooks.com • www.youthlightbooks.com

Dedication

This book is dedicated to the two loves of my life:

Liz, who is beyond quantification—
you are my strength, my support, and my confidant. I love you.

Ella, my newborn daughter;
I pray that I can give you a world that is measured in joy and laughter.

Acknowledgments

I'd like to take the time to thank the many people who helped me put this book together: First to Bob Bowman, who pushed me to refine, rewrite, and rethink so much; I am so grateful for your input. I do not know of many publishing company presidents that would work so closely with a first time writer.

To four counselors that took the time to proof lessons, to pilot lessons, and to show me which parts were going right, which sections were going wrong, and what components needed to change. To Jenni Briggs, Lisa King, Steven Otten, and Kathryn Strother, I cannot thank you enough for being part of this process.

I'd like to thank Cheryl Bacon, Instructional Coach, at my elementary school for letting me stay in her office and ask her question after question about gathering data. You were a key to bringing these lessons to reality and your suggestions were what elevated an okay lesson to a good lesson and a good lesson to a great lesson.

Thanks to Matt Garrett and Nicole Pfleger for doing the nit-picky work. You helped cross the T's and dot the I's. It's a tough job and I'm so thankful that both of you did it.

Thanks to Dr. Colleen Morich for helping clean up the assessments. Your last minute suggestions were incredibly helpful for making more effective and concise questions. A good lesson only gets better with good assessment. Thank you!

I would especially like to thank Dr. Trish Hatch for her guidance and teachings on how to create great measurement questions. The information you taught in your workshops and in your book *Evidence-Based School Counseling* are helping to change school counseling for the better.

A big thanks to Susan Bowman, too. Your keen eye at the end of this writing process was so helpful. Next time I'll make sure to make the font bigger so I don't strain your eyes on the rough draft! I'm glad that we could collaborate together so close to publication.

Thanks to all the teachers who pulled me up when a lesson was in the initial stage. When the activity wasn't going well, you found a way to still make it count. As each lesson went from classroom to classroom, it got better and better. Your "on–the-spot-editing" kept me from becoming overwhelmed and frustrated. Thanks to each and every one of you. I couldn't work with a better group of teachers.

And finally thank you to the Cobb County counselors. Your advocacy and dedication to students is an inspiration day in and day out. You all are the best!

Table of Contents

Introduction

We know that we make a difference. Now we can show our impact!

Guidance with Good Measure exists because our profession is evolving into a data-driven practice. Many counselors are intimidated by the idea that they are asked to collect quantifiable information. How do you quantify lessons on character? How do you measure whether or not a student "got it" from a counseling lesson?

This book will provide you with 25 lessons that answer those questions. Based on the American School Counselor Association's academic, social/emotional, and career standards, *Guidance with Good Measure* can easily be integrated into any school counseling program.

Whether you are using these lessons for classroom activities or a small group, each lesson is designed to be interactive, thought provoking, and fun. But, perhaps more integral, is that each lesson can challenge the students to assess their understanding.

There are several positive reasons for using assessments. First, when students know that there will be a "test," there is a greater motivation to listen. Second, when the assessment is given, the standards that were taught are reinforced since the students have to read and think about what they experienced. The assessments help the students anchor the most important components of the lessons in their minds. Finally, data acquired can be used as a method for further instruction.

As you start using the lessons within, you are opening up your counseling program to a new array of possibilities. Whether you are a first time counselor who could benefit from standard-based lessons or you are a veteran counselor who would like to energize your program into a data driven model, there is something for every counselor here!

Rationale

This book will provide you with resources to integrate accountability into your counseling program. As we enter a more data driven era of education, there is a call for more than qualitative stories of how the counselor impacted the student body. With mandates coming from national and state legislators to show educational impact, school counselors have become part of the discussion regarding their ability to make a difference (Dahir & Stone, 2007). Our profession has to become more than "feel good stories." It is imperative to show that we are closely connected with the success of our students. Can we teach conflict resolution? Can we prove the students grasped the concept of intrinsic versus extrinsic motivation? Can we show how students understand what it means to exercise delayed gratification? These are the questions, and the myriad of others similar to them, that have become a part of our professional dialogue.

Guidance with Good Measure is designed as a developmental tool for collecting data. For 25 years, our literature has called for greater accountability (Nims, James, & Hughley, 1998); this text exists as a response to those calls. Each lesson is written with the goal of gaining information about the students once the lesson is complete.

These lessons, in essence, then become action research. Counselors have shown in the literature that they can bring their findings down to earth and can make immediate and targeted use of this data (Issacs, 2003). Perhaps the information indicates that a small number of students did not understand the lesson taught—the data may then drive the counselor to form a small group. Perhaps the information indicates that nearly the whole classroom shows comprehension of the lesson—this data then could drive the counselor to spend more time on areas of weakness.

If, according to the literature, there are certain stakeholders in education that view school counseling as fiscally irresponsible and a poor use of resources (Whiston, 2002), then our profession should do all in its power to address this concern. When we can leave a classroom or a small group with evidence of our work, we empower ourselves to show others that we make a difference. School Counselors need to become advocates of the profession; by holding ourselves accountable and taking that extra step toward data-driven practices, we can make others aware of the impact our programs make in the lives of students (Curry & Lambie, 2007).

As counselors, we know that we are making a difference. Our careers are about helping others and creating change. We are a profession of advocates that touch the hearts and minds of students. We inspire. We connect.

Guidance with Good Measure offers us opportunities to use data to further help us make an impact. The lessons and assessments within this book offer us opportunities to show others the difference that we make.

Data Collection: Three Styles

"Take your gains where you can get them."
Robert Myrick, author of A Practical Guide to School Counseling

Counselors are busy—to say otherwise would be, if you excuse the data language, erroneous. The thought of going from a counseling program that does little to no data collection to a full on data-driven practice can be intimidating. So, before going any further, it may be important to point out that any step forward in data collection is a *positive step forward.*

Data Collection for the every day school counselor can be broken down into three categories. It may be helpful to think of where you are currently with your program and what kind of information you wish to acquire from your students. In this section, we will briefly discuss the categories and the benefits for each.

Light Data Collection

Light data collection is for a counselor who is ready to start a data driven practice, but does not have the time to run a full scale program. Using this method, the counselor is beginning to integrate some assessments; the counselor may use the assessments primarily as lesson reinforcement and as a decision making tool secondarily. Light data collection, as an example, might be shown to the administration as evidence of the counselor's program.

Moderate Data Collection

Moderate data collection is for a counselor who may want to present information to the staff, use their data for job accountability, or perhaps, give their findings to the district level as evidence of the impact the counselor's program is making. Using this method entails the counselor to focus diligently on distributing assessments for every activity, monitoring levels of change, and using the data to further propel their program. Essentially, the counselor lets the student's information dictate what their program should do next.

Heavy Data Collection

Heavy data collection is for the counselor who is looking at publication, grant writing or graduate level work. Heavy data collection will use an intensive incorporation of assessments into their daily program. This includes running pre and post test groups and using more explicit statistical analysis beyond taking class averages (i.e, finding variance, level of correlation, using the alpha coefficient) to show levels of impact. Light and Moderate data collection may be considered the "down and dirty" information whereas Heavy data collection will be examined and refined to publication standards.

No matter where you are in your counseling program, initiating data collection is a positive step. Whether keeping it simple or using something more intricate, the changes you make in your program are going to be beneficial.

In the concluding section of this introduction, we will briefly go over some methods for measurement—these are quick, simple ways for processing information. The methods are directed to those incorporating the *Light* or *Moderate* styles of data collection.

Methods of Measurement

What Happens Now?

So you've completed your lesson, distributed your assessment, and collected the data. What needs to happen now? Processing your data will be an integral part of showing what has occurred during your time in the classroom. Did your students understand the concepts? Can they replicate the methods taught? Do they even believe that what you are teaching them are realistic and effective techniques? All of these questions can be answered when looking at the students' data.

Here are four methods of data presentation—three are for the quantifiable measurements; one is for the student-centric data.

1. **Per Student Assessment**

   This is the equivalent to grading papers. When examining data, the student's assessments are scored on an individual basis. Looking at each students understanding of the concepts can be used to see who may need extra help. A presentation may look like this:

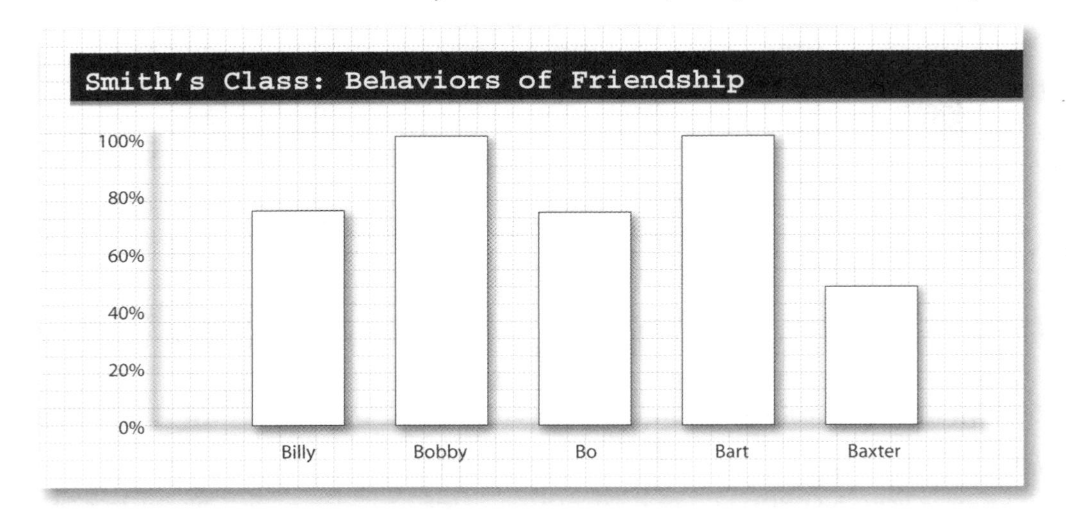

   In this method, you can see which students understand the concepts taught and which students may need further assistance—perhaps they would benefit from a small group on the subject.

2. **Per Classroom Assessment**

   Using the classroom presentation is helpful for recognizing the overall success of a lesson based on *classroom averages*. This information is helpful in observing grade-wide trends: Was the lesson effective overall? Does this lesson need to be re-taught? What needs to change to make a greater impact? A presentation may look like this:

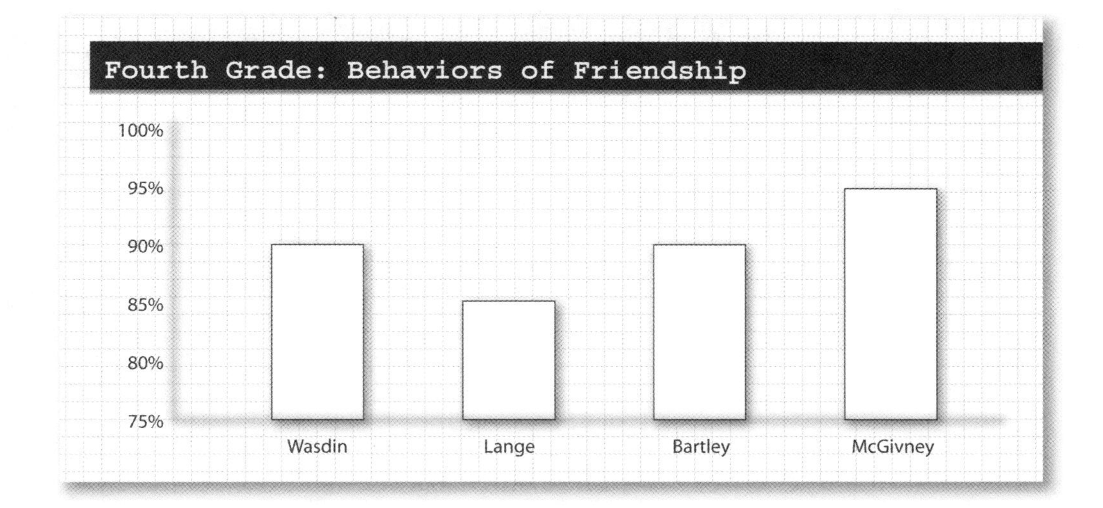

Using a grade-wide presentation may be helpful for showing administrators how entire classrooms respond to the delivery of the lessons.

3. **Per School Assessment**
School assessments are similar to the classroom assessment, but based on the *average of the whole grade level.* Presenting data in this method can show school-wide program integration. A presentation may look like this:

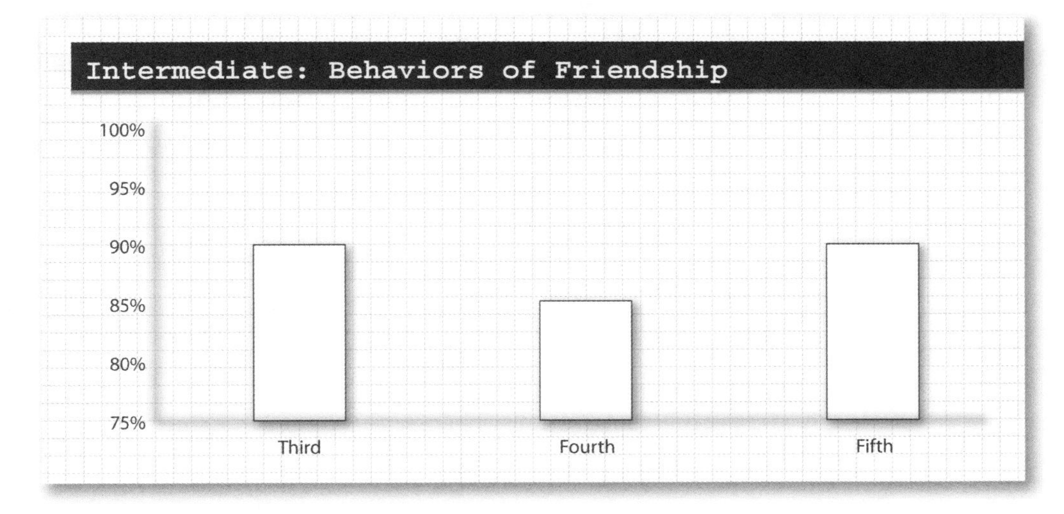

4. **Student-Centric Data**
Student-centric data can be important because it shows a more introspective viewpoint of information. Various lesson activities can be used to recognize themes that need to be explored further. Data may be presented as follows:

Concerns and Resources (Kane's 5th Grade Class)

Name	Type of Conflict	How Stressful? 1 = low, 5 = high	Who is your resource?
Sally	Friend	5	Teacher
Steven	Friend	4	Myself
Sonja	Family	3	???
Shantall	Friend	5	Peers
Skip	Family	4	Myself

Looking at this information, we see that Sally, Steven, and Shantall feel stressed out when there are conflicts between friends but they see different resources as an effective way to deal with that stress. Perhaps these students could collaborate to create a list of strategies that they may not have thought of individually.

Sonja and Skip both are stressed out by Family Conflict. Notice that Sonja didn't respond to who her resource should be and Skip indicated that he would attempt to solve his own familial conflicts. Should fifth graders solve their own problems when it comes to family? What if the conflicts involve some type of major change that is beyond Skip's control? Why does Sonja not identify a resource to help her out? These students may benefit from working together and making a realistic plan of action for conflict that arises in the family.

As you can see, the data can be helpful for multiple reasons. It can help in developing small groups, evaluating the impact of the delivery, and presenting information to administrators and others. No matter the purpose of the presentation, the important key is this: No presentation is possible unless there is data and evidence!

Guidance with Good Measure—Lesson Descriptions

Each lesson is written for maximum clarity and efficiency. Each lesson will consist of the following:

• **Materials:**	The items that you will need to recreate the lesson.
• **Overview:**	The primary focus, or essential question, that the lesson will achieve.
• **ASCA Standards:**	For those who follow the American School Counseling Association model of delivery—the skills that will be incorporated in the lesson. *Supplemental standards for the lesson are italicized.*
• **Procedure:**	The directions of the lesson—this ranges from the"rule of the game" (should a game be played) to a set of discussion questions that can be used to springboard conversation.
• Data:	Will indicate what type of data will be available from using the assessment. It may be quantifiable, student-centric, and many times, both. This section also indicates the answers to the assessments, the point value for the questions, and other information that will be helpful in data collection. *Guidance with Good Measure* sets a standard of 90% success with each lesson. Counselors not using the 90th percentile should consider at what percentage point they would recognize that their students "got" the lesson.

• **Optional Lesson Extensions:**	Want to go beyond the basic lesson? Here are some ideas that can extend and vary your delivery. *Guidance with Good Measure* also will indicate various books, data collection techniques, and other information in this area.
• **Assessment:**	The assessment to be delivered at the end of the lesson. Each assessment is relatively short, but still incorporating the skills and indicators taught during the class.
• **Reproducible:**	A copy of the reproducible that will be distributed to the students.

How to Implement the Lessons

Guidance with Good Measure has a simple, concise format that is easy to follow. Each lesson begins with the overview, ASCA standards, materials, and approximate time for each lesson. The procedures are outlined in step by step fashion. Following the procedures are the assessment answers, optional lesson extensions and then the assessment. Reproducible pages can be found at the end of each lesson.

A successful lesson will have the school counselor going through the procedures using the reproducible pages where needed. At the conclusion of the lesson, the students will be given the quick assessment which can then easily be used for data collection, reporting purposes, and information as to how to drive instruction.

Section One:

Name: ______________________________ **Date:** ____________________

1 2 3 4 5 6 7 8 9 10 11

Academic Domain

The Game of Life

Overview

Students will realize that preparation and patience can lead to satisfactory results.

ASCA Standards

- AD.C1.6: Understand how school success and academic achievement enhance future career and vocational opportunities
- CD.C1.1: *Understand the relationship between educational achievement and career success*
- CD.C1.5: *Describe the effect of work on lifestyle*
- PS.B1.2: *Understand consequences of decisions and choices*

Materials

Play Money
Delayed Gratification Assessment
Gang/Professional Cards

Approximate Time: 45 minutes

Procedures

1. If the students are not in groups, place them into at least four groups.
2. Ask the class if they have ever heard the words "Delayed Gratification." Take some hypotheses as to what the students think. Explain to the students that delayed gratification is the ability to wait for a reward. Ask the question, "What would you enjoy more: a cup of popcorn kernels or a big bowl of popcorn?" "Can you think of anything else that involves delayed gratification?"
3. Discuss that patience is an important component of delayed gratification. When students can calmly wait, they are exhibiting patience.
   a. What are some ways to be patient?
   b. When are some times to be patient?

4. Explain that delayed gratification happens all the time in life and today the students are going to get to experience the difference between people who "want it now" and people who "want to wait." Half of the groups will be GANG MEMBERS and the other half will be PEOPLE IN CAREERS.
5. Distribute CAREER cards to half of the groups and GANG cards to the other groups.
6. The Game of Life will be played in 5 rounds where each round represents one year of time—after each round, if the questions are answered appropriately, the groups will be rewarded with their salary. The counselor will play the role of the banker and distribute money following each round.
7. Also in life, there are police officers; the teacher will represent the **police officer**. *(His/her job is to come and confiscate the gang members money in rounds* **2 and 5** to show the results of profiting in an illegal way.)
8. On the back of the CAREER and GANG cards is information regarding how much money is made for each "year" of the game—those in careers make various amounts of money, but often make very little in the first two to three rounds of the game because they are receiving their education. GANG member groups make ten dollars per year.
9. The following questions are asked per round. There are GANG and CAREER questions:

   Round 1 — **Gang Question 1:** Why do people join gangs? **Career Question 1:** What do people need to do to get into college?

   Round 2 — **Gang Question 2:** What do gang members do to make money? **Career Question 2:** What do you think are some benefits of graduating high school and/or college? *(Police confiscate money from "gang members")*

   Round 3 — **Gang Question 3:** How would your family feel if you joined a gang? **Career Question 3:** How would your family feel if you got the career you always wanted to have?

   Round 4 — **Gang Question 4:** How does a gang affect the community? **Career Question 4:** How does a person in a successful career affect the community?

   Round 5 — **Gang Question 5:** What can happen to gang members? **Career Question 5:** What do you think helps people in careers have success? *(Police confiscate money from "gang members")*

10. At the end of the 5 "years" ask the following discussion questions:
    a. Who had more money during the first few rounds of the game? Why?
    b. What happened as those groups with the career cards got out of college?
    c. How can delaying gratification help you while you are in school?

Data

Quantitative: 90% of the students will understand what delayed gratification is and the positive benefits of patience.

Answers for the Delayed Gratification Assessment:

1. B
2. D
3. A
4. A
5. C

Total points for assessment: 5

Optional Lesson Extension

(adding five to ten minutes to a lesson)

1. **Real World Information**—Share the following information as a lead-in to the activity:

Level of Education	How much you make on average in one week
Doctoral degree	$1,441
Professional degree	$1,474
Master's degree	$1,140
Bachelor's degree	$962
Associate degree	$721
Some college, no degree	$674
High-school graduate	$595
Less than a high school diploma	$419

Information from the U.S. Department of Labor http://www.bls.gov/emp/emptab7.htm

2. **Real World**—Have the students share their times when they used delayed gratification in school and at home. What did the students do? What did the students say to themselves?

Name: ______________________________ Date: ________________

Delayed Gratification Assessment

1. **What does delayed gratification mean?**
   a. When someone gets on your nerves and makes you mad
   b. Taking the time to receive the best reward
   c. Missing out on a reward because you waited too long to act
   d. Waiting around to talk to a teacher because you got upset
   e. Being on your best behavior all the time

2. **Which student is using delayed gratification?**
   a. Sam plays all day because it is more fun than studying
   b. Susan shouts all the answers out in class because she wants to be first
   c. Shaun eats his popcorn snack first because it is his favorite
   d. Senica gets to use the whole recess time because she finished her homework first
   e. Steven races to the front of the line to be the first

3. **Some jobs that pay well can only be earned by people who go to college. Why?**
   a. Because people are being trained for a special task
   b. Because people have to learn how to cheat and get rich
   c. Because certain jobs want you to be older before you work for them
   d. Because people in college should be given a lot of money
   e. None of the above

4. **How could you use patience?**
   a. To calmly wait for your turn
   b. To share something with a friend
   c. To take something without asking for it
   d. To tell someone that you want something
   e. To give something to someone

5. **Who earns the most money?**
   a. People who steal and cheat
   b. People who drop out of high school
   c. People who finish college
   d. They all earn the same
   e. None of the above

Career and Gang Cards (front)

Directions: Copy front and back of cards onto two-sided page for activity. Trim and distribute.

Lawyer: I help people understand the law.	**Counselor:** I help people identify feelings and achieve goals.
Teacher: I help students learn.	**Surgeon:** I fix people's bodies when they get hurt.
Gang Member: I don't care if I hurt other people's feelings.	**Gang Member:** If I don't get what I want, I get mad.

Career and Gang Cards (back)

Year 1: College, $0
Year 2: Got a job, $20
Year 3: Working hard, $40
Year 4: A veteran at what I do, $60
Year 5: I love my career! $80

Year 1: I'm in college, $0
Year 2: Law School! $0
Year 3: Got a job! $40
Year 4: Promotion, $80
Year 5: Life is good! $100

Year 1: College! $0
Year 2: Still studying, $0
Year 3: Medical School, $0
Year 4: Got a job! $100
Year 5: I love being a doctor! $140

Year 1: College! $0
Year 2: I'm a teacher! $20
Year 3: I love teaching, $40
Year 4: My job is great! $60
Year 5: I'm glad I stayed in school, $80

Year 1: $10
Year 2: $10
Year 3: $10
Year 4: $10
Year 5: $10

Year 1: $10
Year 2: $10
Year 3: $10
Year 4: $10
Year 5: $10

Don't Hide Your Pride

Overview

Students will recognize how their attitude toward school and their school work will affect their education.

ASCA Standards

- AD.A1.2: Display a positive interest in learning
- AD.A1.3: Take pride in work and achievement

Materials

Respect and Pride Assessment
Respect and Pride Role Play Cards
Scenario Cards
Character Outcomes

Approximate Time: 30 minutes

Procedures

1. Divide the class into small groups.
2. Explain to the students: The way we behave in class has a direct impact on our achievement. When kids show pride in their work, then they are more likely to succeed. When kids show apathy toward what they do, it is reflected in their work.
   a. How can you tell if you are showing pride in your work?
   b. How can you tell if your behavior is helping you achieve your academic goals?
3. Distribute the Respect and Pride Role Play Cards to the groups. Here are the following "parts:"
   a. The Engaged Learner: The person who is involved and tries
   b. The Doubting Learner: The person who thinks their work is never good enough

   c. The Lack-of-Interest Learner: The person who shrugs and nods to avoid answering questions
   d. The La-La-Land Learner: The person who goofs off and thinks that the whole day of school is a play time
   e. The Off-Topic Learner: The person who wants to only talk about one subject (Sports, Music, etc) and shows no interest unless it is about their favorite subject

4. Each group will then act out a scenario; the rest of the class will have to guess which role the individual students played. The counselor will read the scenario to the class to "set up the scene."
5. After the students guess which roles were played by whom, the class must predict what will happen to the students.
   a. After predictions, those in the role play will read the "How the Story Ends" portion of their card to tell what ended up happening to their characters.
      - After the events transpired, which characters had success?
      - Which characters would have an undesirable outcome?
6. Discussion Questions:
   a. How did behavior impact performance?
   b. How does it feel to succeed? Why might some people not take pride in their work?
   c. If you were not happy with your academic performance, what steps could you take to change?
   d. When you display interest in your school work, what are potential outcomes?
7. Distribute the Respect and Pride Assessment.

Data

Quantitative: 90% of the students will be able to identify how behavior impacts performance; students will indicate the importance of taking pride in their work.

Answers to the Respect and Pride Assessment:

1. C
2. C
3. E
4. E
5. C

Total points for assessment: 5

Optional Lesson Extensions

(adding five to ten minutes to a lesson)

1. **Self-Assessment**—Have the students write down what kind of learner in the classroom they think they are; have them describe if that is the type of learner they want to be and what they need to do to change. If they are happy with the type of learner they are, have them indicate what they should do to maintain their learning style.
2. **Find in Text**—Have the students discuss which characters from various books fit into the different roles; what happens to those characters in their stories?

Name: ______________________ **Date:** ______________

Respect and Pride Assessment

1. **Which of the following statements is true?**
   - a. My behavior has nothing to do with my grades
   - b. I do not get to choose how I behave
   - c. My behavior is connected to my grades
   - d. When I show pride in school, it won't make a difference on my grades
   - e. The only way to make good grades is to be smart and lucky
   - f. None of the above
2. **Edward normally makes "C"s in Social Studies. He tried a bit harder and got a "B" on his latest test. Which statement is NOT helpful?**
   - a. "Alright! I tried harder and earned a better grade"
   - b. "My grades are improving and that feels great"
   - c. "Everyone else made better grades and they are smarter then me"
   - d. "Making a "B" is okay and I want to make an "A" next time"
   - e. "I know that I can keep up this work level, it's not so hard"
3. **What happens if you show interest in many subjects?**
   - a. You will gain information that can be used from subject to subject
   - b. All of your grades might improve
   - c. You will feel like every part of the school day is worth your time
   - d. You will set a good example for other classmates
   - e. All of the above
4. **How can you show pride in your school work?**
   - a. Attempting all assignments, even if they are difficult
   - b. Keeping a positive attitude about school
   - c. Trying to find something you like about each subject
   - d. Having good behavior in the classroom
   - e. All of the above
5. **Which learner will have the best chance of success?**
   - a. The La-La-Land Learner
   - b. The Doubting Learner
   - c. The Engaged Learner
   - d. The Off-Topic Learner
   - e. The Lack-of-Interest Learner

Role Play Cards

Directions: Cut and distribute to student groups. Students will role-play the type of learner card they receive.

The Engaged Learner:

The person who is involved and tries

The Doubting Learner:

The person who thinks their work is never good enough

The Lack-of-Interest Learner:

The person who shrugs and nods to avoid answering questions

The La-La-Land Learner:

The person who goofs off and thinks that the whole day of school is a play time

The Off-Topic Learner:

The person who wants to only talk about one subject (Sports, Music, etc) and shows no interest unless it is about their favorite subject

Scenario Cards

Directions: Distribute one scenario per group. The students will role-play their scenario while the rest of the class will try to guess which type of learner each student is.

The students are going over the spelling homework.

The students are learning about a new book the whole class will read.

The students have to divide up responsibilities for a project.

The students are studying together for a test.

The students are trying to come up with activities for the school talent show.

The students are outside learning about different plants for Science.

The students are trying to come up with a way to redecorate the classroom.

Name of Students in the Group:

____

Date: ____________________

Respect and Pride Group Character Outcomes

Write a sentence about what ended up happening to the different characters.

1. **How did the story end for the Engaged Learner?**

____

____

____

2. **How did the story end for the Doubtful Learner?**

____

____

____

3. **How did the story end for the Lack-of-Interest Learner?**

____

____

____

4. **How did the story end for the La-La-Land Learner?**

____

____

____

5. **How did the story end for the Off-Topic Learner?**

____

____

Focus!

Overview

Students will be able to identify methods of staying focused; students will be able to recognize the importance of keeping track of what needs to be accomplished.

ASCA Standards

- AD.A3.2: Demonstrate the ability to work independently, as well as the ability to work cooperatively with other students
- PS.A1.8: *Understand the need for self-control and how to practice it*

Materials

Nerf-like balls (at least three)
On-Task Assessment

Approximate Time: 30 minutes

Procedures

1. Introduce the lesson: "Today we are going to talk about the variety of ways that it can be difficult to stay on task at school. Can you think of ways that kids get distracted during the school day?" Students may respond with:
   a. Friends joking around
   b. Daydreaming
   c. Being tired
   d. Worrying about something else
2. Explain to the students: No matter what may be distracting us, our success comes from the ability to focus on what needs to be accomplished. When we can stay on track with what we are doing and what needs to be done, we will be much more successful—this takes self-control! Discuss the following ways this can be accomplished.
   a. To joke around with your friends outside of class

b. To remind yourself that it is time to focus
c. To make sure that you are well-rested for school
d. To figure out when you can properly address what is worrying you

3. Have the students form a large circle. Hand out one ball; tell the students that they must throw it to another classmate in the circle—everyone must have a chance to catch and toss the ball.
   a. The students are to throw the ball around the circle by gently tossing it.
   b. The students are to use the same throwing pattern—each student will throw to the same student every time.
   c. After the ball has been passed four or five times, give a new ball to the first student who threw and have him or her throw again while the first ball is still being tossed.
   d. See how many balls can be "involved" in the circle at the same time.

4. When the class makes a mistake—either with an errant throw or things become too chaotic, address what is happening. Some discussion questions:
   a. What is causing the distraction?
   b. What are ways that we can be more successful in this activity?
   c. What are the most important aspects of this activity for you to focus on?

5. Explain that success will come when individual students can show the self-control to **pay attention to what is going on** (trying to catch the ball) and **what needs to be done** (making a good throw to the next person).
   a. Ask: How are the goals of this activity similar to events that occur in the school day?
   b. **Indicate that we are more likely to make mistakes when we focus on other events rather than the task at hand.**

6. Conclude by distributing the On-Task Assessment.

Data

Quantitative: 90% of the students will be able to identify the importance of staying on task; students will be able to indicate appropriate methods of staying focused.

Answers to the On-Task Assessment:

1. E
2. B,E
3. A
4. B
5. E

Total points for assessment: 6

Optional Lesson Extensions

(adding five to ten minutes to a lesson)

1. **Silent Toss**—When the students are tossing the balls around the circle, tell them for one round that they cannot communicate. In what ways does this help? In what ways does this make the activity more difficult?
2. **Greater Distraction**—When you toss the ball, have the students call the name of another student *who is not supposed to catch the ball* (i.e., if Sam tosses the ball to Juan, he will call out Julie's name instead of Juan's). How are students responsible for making distractions? What can students do to limit distractions during a lesson?

Name: ______________________ Date: ____________

On-Task Assessment

1. **What happens when you are distracted during a lesson?**
   a. It may be difficult to understand what needs to be done
   b. You may become upset at yourself or friends for distracting you
   c. Your grades may not be as good
   d. You may need to take more time figuring out the right way to do the assignments
   e. All of the above
2. **Circle TWO of the answers: What are the keys to staying on-task?**
   a. Pay attention to what others are doing
   b. Pay attention to what I am currently doing
   c. Pay attention to what happened in the last subject
   d. Pay attention to what I'm going to eat for lunch
   e. Pay attention to what needs to be done
   f. Pay attention to how other kids pay attention
   g. Pay attention to what is going on outside
3. **How can you stay focused on a lesson?**
   a. Keep my eyes and ears on the teacher
   b. Look out the window
   c. Think about what I'm going to do when I go home
   d. Talk to my classmate once I understand what to do
   e. Write notes to other kids asking them to help me
   f. None of the above
4. **What does it mean to use self-control during a lesson?**
   a. To make sure the class is on-task
   b. To make sure that I am focused on what I am doing and what needs to be done
   c. To make sure that I understand everything the first time it is taught
   d. To make sure that everyone knows that I am concentrating on getting good grades
   e. To make sure that all my friends are making good choices about focusing
   f. All of the above

5. **What will let you know that you are focused and on-task?**
   a. You have been following the teachers instructions
   b. You understand pretty much what needs to be done
   c. Your thoughts were almost entirely about the lesson
   d. You can describe to others what you learned during the lesson
   e. All of the above

Stacking Up Your Potential

Overview

Students will learn the importance of building an academic foundation for career and social success.

ASCA Standards

- AD.C1.2: Understand the relationship between learning and work
- AD.C1.4: Demonstrate an understanding of the value of life-long learning as essential to seeking, obtaining, and maintaining life goals
- AD.C1.5: Understand that school success is the preparation to make the transition from student to community member
- AD.C1.6: Understand how school success and academic achievement enhance future career and vocational activities

Materials

Stacking Materials (dominos, wooden blocks, or even books)
Building Success Assessment

Approximate Time: 30 minutes

Procedures

1. Place the students in groups of four or five.
2. Ask the students, "How would you build the sturdiest, strongest building?" Take appropriate responses (use strong material, have things measured out, etc.).
3. Explain—"When people build, one of the most important aspects is a strong foundation. This is the bottom part of the building upon which everything else is stacked." Other comments that can be made for part of the conversation:

   a. "The better the foundation, the higher the building can go."
   b. "When we build, our foundations let us add more and more."
4. Distribute sets of blocks (dominos, books, etc) to each table.
5. Ask the students to work together to build two different buildings in their groups: one building that does not have a strong foundation and one that does.
   a. Which building is more likely to fall down?
   b. Which building will be able to endure bad weather?
6. Discuss with the students, "If a foundation for a building is made from strong and durable materials, what "materials" (or skills) would be needed for students to have a foundation that can lead to success?"
   a. Students might say: friends, good grades, love, attention, family support—take all appropriate answers.
7. Discuss further, "So if a building with a strong foundation can build a lot of floors, what can a person with a strong foundation build up?"
   a. Possible answers (or prompts): passing to the next grade, passing tests, getting good jobs, etc.
   b. Create a building representing student success:
      - Build a strong foundation ("This student's foundation is of someone who studies hard, does all his homework, and tries to get along with others.")
      - Then on top of the foundation, stack more blocks ("This block represents Statewide Testing. This next block represents going to the next grade.")
8. Now, have the students work in their groups to tell a story with their structure—let the students decide what kind of success they want to stack on top of the foundation. This might be passing to the next grade, going to college, becoming a successful professional, etc.
9. When the students are done with their buildings, have each table share the "story" of their building.
10. Conclude by distributing the Building Success Assessment.

Data

Quantitative: 90% of the students will be able to identify the importance of the building and usefulness of a strong foundation.

Answers for the Building Success Assessment:

1. B
2. D
3. A
4. E
5. Completed "building" with appropriate foundation and goals (2 points)

Total points for assessment: 7

Optional Lesson Extensions

(adding five to ten minutes to a lesson)

1. Create some "stressors" to affect the students' buildings—ask the students what are some things that might try to knock down a group's building.
   a. Try to lightly knock over one of the buildings by indicating the stress/conflict.
      - Say, "Now comes along peer pressure. What will happen to someone with a strong foundation? What will happen to a person who does not have it?"
2. Take volunteers and have them be classroom examples—one student will have a strong foundation and one student will not have a strong foundation.
3. Ask students to think of historical figures that have strong foundations—
   What characteristics did they have that would show their ability to become successful?

Name: ______________________ **Date:** ______________

Building Success Assessment

1. What is a strong *student* foundation?

a. The basement of a building
b. Skills that help you reach your goals
c. Kids who pressure you to dress in a certain way
d. Passing the statewide tests
e. None of the above

2. What is NOT an example of a foundation?

a. Working well with others
b. Good behavior
c. Listening and following directions
d. Eating your lunch quickly
e. All of the above

3. Which sentence could a person with a strong foundation say?

a. "I know that doing my homework every night teaches me responsibility for other tasks"
b. "As long as I can be part of a group of friends, I'll be successful with whatever I do"
c. "What I do now has no effect on what I do later on in life"
d. "If I focus and try really hard right now, I still don't think that will help me when I get older"
e. All of the above relate to a successful foundation

4. Why is it important to have a successful foundation?

a. Your foundation helps you with what decisions you will make
b. Your foundation helps you succeed in school
c. Your foundation can help you reach your goals
d. Your foundation can give you a sense of what is right and wrong
e. All of the above

5. **Using six of the words from the word bank, show how a student would have a strong foundation and reach their goals!**

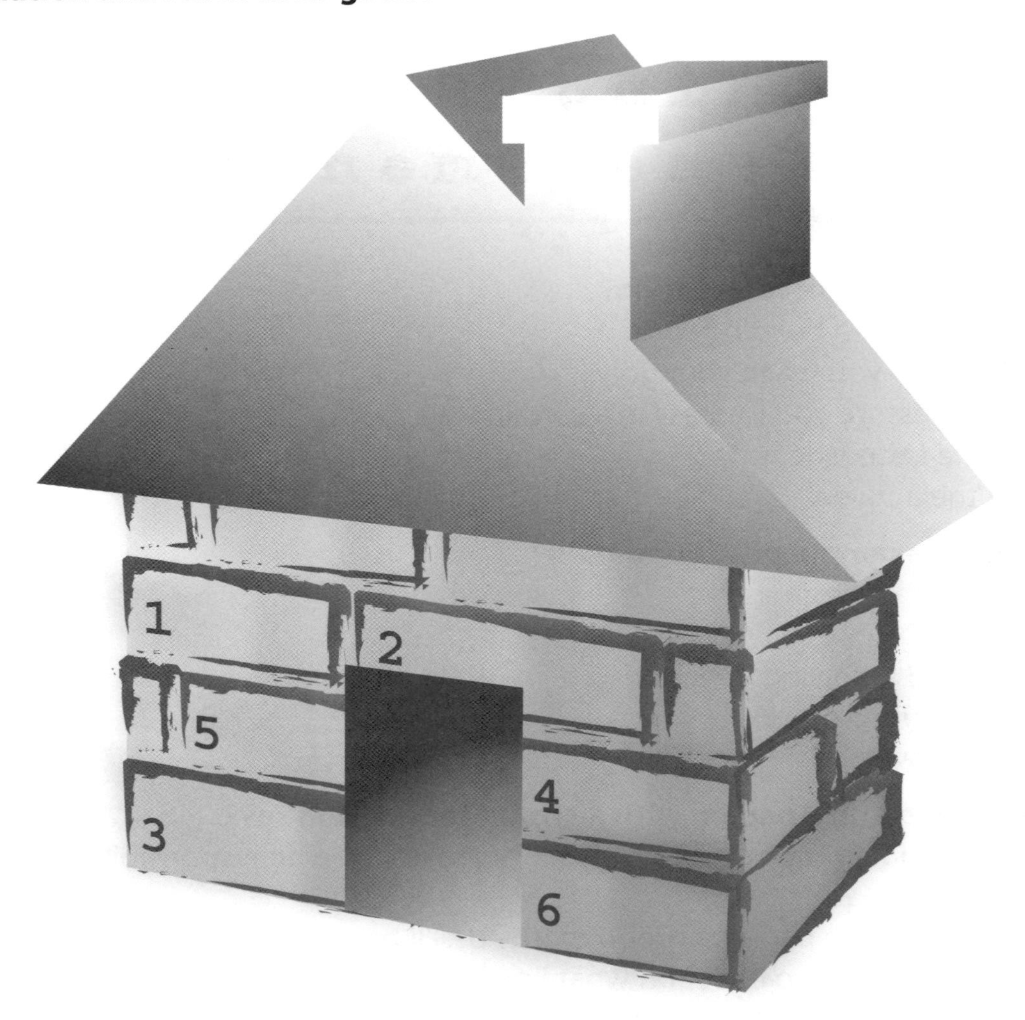

Using time wisely	Making good grades	Giving up	Fighting	Cheating
Passing Tests	Making straight "A's"	Doing homework	Finishing projects	Oversleeping
School success	Getting the job I want	Behaving well	Listening in class	Always arguing
Having school pride	Making good friendships	Teasing students	Lying	Entering College

Using the Past for the Present

Overview

Students will learn how to use previous success to positively affect their present tasks.

ASCA Standards

- AD.A1.5: Identify attitudes and behaviors which lead to successful learning
- AD.A2.4: Apply knowledge and learning styles to positively influence school performance
- AD.B1.6: Use knowledge of learning styles to positively influence school performance

Materials

Connections to the Past Reproducible
Past/Present Assessment

Approximate Time: 30 minutes

Procedures

1. Explain to the students that one key to learning is to find actions, behaviors, and thoughts that have previously brought about success and repeat those in the present situations. For example:
   a. If a student wrote sentences for Social Studies vocabulary (past behavior) and got an "A" on her Social Studies exam (success); she may find the same success if she writes sentences with her Science vocabulary (new challenge) on a Science exam.
2. Distribute to each student the Connections to the Past Reproducible.
   a. The students are to write down the many successes that they have had in the past—it can be anything from learning how to ride a bike to acing a math quiz.
   b. The students are then to write what they did to achieve their success.

c. In the third column, students are to write challenges that they are currently facing—from trouble with friends to confusing school work.
d. Finally, the students are to use the middle column, their methods of achievement, and draw lines connecting which methods would help with new challenges.

3. On the board, it may be helpful to create a classroom model for the students:

I am successful at	Method of Achievement	New Challenges
Football	Work hard	Writing
Reading	Practice over and over again	Multiplication Tables
Science Projects	Go home and work at night	Social Studies

4. Discussion Questions:
   a. How can looking at previous successes show you how you can overcome new challenges?
   b. What do you notice about the "methods of achievement?"
      - They are universal techniques that can help in many situations
   c. How does it feel to know that you already have many keys to success in your history?
   d. What happens if one "method of achievement" does not work? Where can you get more ideas?

5. Distribute the Past/Present Assessment.

Data

Quantitative: 90% of the students will be able to identify why past successes can lead to overcoming present challenges; students will indicate that they know how to use past successes for present challenges.

Answers to the Past/Present Assessment:

1. A
2. B
3. A
4. B

Total points for assessment: 4

Optional Lesson Extensions

(adding five to ten minutes to a lesson)

1. **Get Specific**—Using the model, ask the student to be as specific as possible. If they say, "Work Hard" make sure they indicate what that means. Does it mean spending an hour every night on flash cards? Does it mean reading the newspaper in the morning and looking for vocabulary words?
2. **Make a Plan**—Have the students make a list of challenges that are approaching (tests, try-outs, etc) and create a program of what needs to be done for each.

Name: ____________________ Date: ____________

Past/Present Assessment

1. **How can thinking about your successful actions in the past help you with new challenges?**
   a. You can see what works for you and what does not work for you
   b. You can understand that you should only try what you are good at doing
   c. You can see that everyone must do the same thing when rising to new challenges
   d. You can understand that one success in the past may not help with new challenges
   e. None of the above
2. **You have a new challenge! What question can you ask yourself that may be the most helpful?**
   a. "Why should I try?"
   b. "What have I used before that works for me?"
   c. "How am I going to learn all these new strategies?"
   d. "Who will do my work for me?"
   e. None of the above
3. **What is "studying when I get home from school?"**
   a. A method of achievement
   b. A success
   c. A challenge
   d. All of the above
   e. None of the above
4. **If my new challenge is nothing like my old success, then:**
   a. There is nothing I can do
   b. I can use what I know about succeeding and apply that to my new challenge
   c. I will never succeed in my new challenge
   d. I can hope that I succeed by pure luck
   e. None of the above

Name: ______________________________ **Date:** ____________________

Connections to the Past

Directions: Write down what you are successful at! Then write how you got that way in the Methods of Achievement section. Next, make a list of New Challenges. Draw a line from your Methods of Achievement to your New Challenges. This will show you how to use your past skills to conquer your New Challenges!

I am successful at...	Method of Achievement	New Challenges

The Self-attitudes Platitudes

Overview

Students will learn how to identify self-attitudes that inhibit success. Students will learn how to change negative statements into positive reinforcing statements.

ASCA Standards

- AD.A1.5: Identify attitudes and behaviors which lead to successful learning
- AD.B1.1: Demonstrate the motivation to achieve individual potential
- PS.A1.1: *Develop positive attitudes toward self as a unique and worthy person*

Materials

Self-attitudes Assessment
Self-attitudes Character Sheet
Self-attitudes Statement Correction Activity
Writing Board (or large sheet of paper) and markers

Approximate Time: 30 minutes

Procedures

1. On the marker board or a large piece of paper, draw the following diagram:

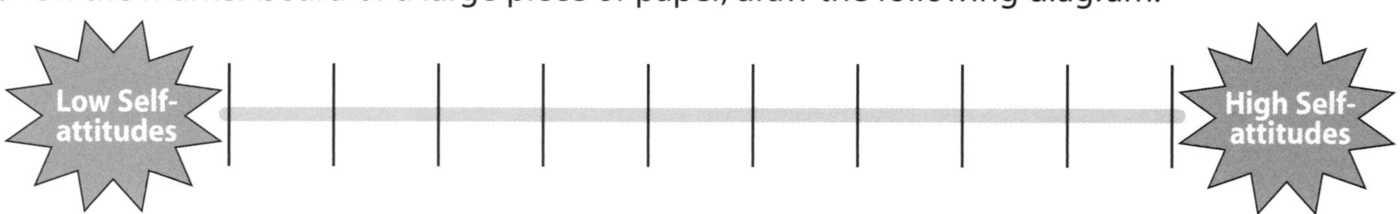

Self-attitudes is made of images, concepts (thoughts), and esteem (feelings)

2. Explain to the students that in today's lesson, the students will learn about self-attitudes. Self-attitudes are the concepts, feelings, and images that a student believes he or she is like. Some students have strong self-attitudes. They feel good about themselves, they think positive thoughts, and they have a positive image of who they are as a person.
   a. Discuss self-image: the way students see themselves. Ask students to identify self-images. Some examples:
      - Some students see themselves as pretty
      - Some students see themselves as overweight
      - Some students see themselves as wimpy
   b. Discuss self-concepts: the way students think about school, events, and everything in between. Ask the students to identify self-concepts. Some examples:
      - Some students think they will never have any friends
      - Some students think they are very funny
      - Some students think they are dumb
   c. Discuss self-esteem: the way students feel about themselves. Some examples:
      - Some students are happy
      - Some students are always sad
      - Some students seem to be angry all of the time
3. Read a list of statements and thoughts that students have from time to time about their self-attitudes. Discuss the area to which it relates. Have the classroom decide where on the scale it should go:
   a. Self-image: Students will first listen to kids talking about their self-image.
      - Self-image Sally thinks, "I would be pretty if I had better clothes."
      - Self-image Steve says, "I like the way my hair looks today."
   b. Self-concepts: Students will listen to kids talking about their self-concepts.
      - Self-concept Carl says, "I can never do anything right at school."
      - Self-concept Christina thinks, "If I try hard enough, I get it right."
   c. Self-esteem: Students will listen to kids talking about their self-esteem.
      - Self-esteem Ella thinks, "Some days are great days, other days are not so great."
      - Self-esteem Ernest thinks, "There is nothing good about anything, ever!"
4. Discuss with the class how words and thoughts have incredible power. If students say or think a certain way long enough, then they will start to believe it!
5. Distribute the self-attitudes character sheet. Explain to the class they are going to read some statements made by different students and decide if they will have high self-attitudes or low self-attitudes.
   a. The students are to draw a line from the characters face to the area on the scale they believe the student belongs.
   b. The students are to correct negative self-attitudes statements to make them more positive and motivational.

6. After the students complete the self-attitudes character sheet, ask the following discussion questions:
    a. How can the way you feel affect your grades? Potential answers:
        - When kids are sad they don't want to do work.
        - Kids who are in good moods like being at school.
    b. What can someone say who has a good self-image? Potential answers:
        - I like myself.
        - I care about myself.
        - I am an important person.
    c. What is a negative self-concept? How could you change it into a positive? Potential answers:
        - Negative: I am dumb and a failure. Positive: I can succeed if I try.
        - Negative: Nobody cares about what I do. Positive: I know that someone is interested in what I do and who I am.
7. Conclude the lesson by distributing the self-attitudes assessment.

Data

Quantitative: 90% of the students will be able to identify attitudes and behavior that lead to successful learning. Students will indicate ways to say positive, motivational statements.

Answers for Self-attitudes Assessment:

1. C
2. B
3. C
4. B
5. C

Total points for assessment: 5

Optional Lesson Extension

(adding five to ten minutes to a lesson)

Find the positive—Students are to look in text books, quote books, or on the internet and make a list of positive quotes that they can use to replace negative thoughts. Students can then discuss what those positive quotes mean to them.

Name: ______________________ Date: ______________

Self-attitudes Assessment

1. **Which statement represents someone who has high self-attitudes:**
   a. I'm just going to fail, no matter what I do
   b. Everyone else can succeed, but I can't
   c. I thought this was impossible, but it's really not
   d. If I don't have someone help me, I'll get confused
   e. Nobody understands, so why should I even try

2. **How do your personal thoughts connect to your behaviors?**
   a. Thoughts and behaviors are not connected
   b. The way I think about myself will impact the way I act
   c. If I think positively, I will probably have negative behavior
   d. If I think negatively, I will most likely have positive behavior
   e. None of the above

3. **What makes up the way that people think about themselves?**
   a. Self-image
   b. Self-esteem
   c. Self-concept
   d. All of the above
   e. None of the above

4. **What is a self-image?**
   a. They way people feel about things
   b. The way people see themselves
   c. The way people think about things
   d. The way people talk to their friends
   e. None of the above

5. **Sam says, "I am going to have a great day!" Is this:**
   a. Self-image
   b. Self-esteem
   c. Self-concept
   d. Self-insults
   e. None of the above

Name: ______________________ Date: ____________

Self-attitudes Character Sheet

Rating Self-attitude Statements

Directions: Looking at the statements below, rate the students' statements on the self-attitudes scale. Write the number that relates to each student on the line below student's statement.

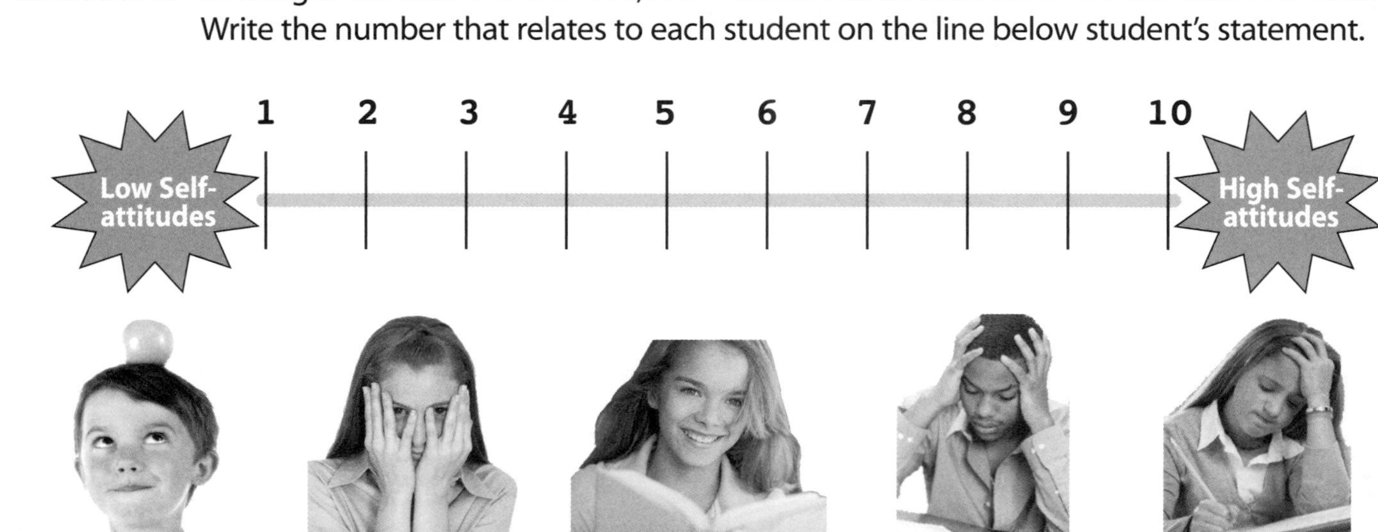

Sean	Sarah	Sally	Shawn	Shelly
"I'm capable of figuring out this stuff."	"I wish that I didn't look this way."	"I think things are going to be okay."	"I don't know how to do math."	"Nothing will ever go my way."
________	________	________	________	________

Changing Self-attitudes Statements

Directions: Read the self-attitudes statements and rewrite them in a more positive and helpful way.

1. Self-image statement: **No matter how I dress, I look really bad.**

   Write how you would change it here:

   ____

   ____

   ____

2. Self-concept statement: **Everything I do is wrong.**

Write how you would change it here:

___

___

___

3. Self-esteem statement: **I know I'm going to feel awful today.**

Write how you would change it here:

___

___

___

Fill Your Bucket

Overview

Students will recognize that their self-talk can impact their academic performance.

ASCA Standards

- AD.A1.5: Identify attitudes and behaviors which lead to successful learning
- PS.A1.1: *Develop a positive attitude toward self as a unique and worthy person*

Materials

Bucket or Container
Feathers, note cards, or anything light weight
Wooden Blocks, Books, or rocks
Self-Talk Reproducible
Self-Talk Assessment

Approximate Time: 30 minutes

Procedures

1. Have two students come to the front of the classroom and demonstrate two different scenarios:
   a. What do you think a student looks like who is constantly saying awful things to themselves? (Have the first volunteer show the following behaviors)
      - The student may walk with their head down.
      - The student may drag their feet.
      - They may slump their shoulders.

   b. What do you think a student looks like who is constantly saying positive words to themselves? (Have the second volunteer show the following behaviors)
      - Student may walk with their head high.

- Student may walk with a skip in their step.
- They might be smiling a lot.

2. Say, "When we fill our minds with negative thoughts, it is like we are putting bricks [heavy books, rocks] in our head!"
   a. Invite another volunteer to the front of the class and hand them a bucket. (It may even help to draw a face on the bucket). Ask them to pretend that they are constantly filling their mind with negative words. Ask the students, what are some of the negative words kids might say to themselves?
      - I can't do it.
      - This it too hard.
      - I'll never get done.
   b. For every time that the student says a negative statement, add the heavy object into the bucket.
   c. Ask the class, "What did you notice about a student who is filling their mind with negative thoughts? What do you think might happen when the student is challenged with learning something new at school?"

3. Say, "When we fill our mind with positive sayings and thoughts, it is like we are filling our mind with light, easy to carry things!"
   a. Invite another student to the front of the class. This time have them hold the bucket. Ask the class to give examples of positive words or sayings that can go in the bucket.
      - This is easy.
      - If I try a little bit harder, I can do it.
      - I can succeed!
   b. Ask, "What did you notice about the student with positive thoughts? What would happen if this student were to have something new to learn at school?"

4. Explain: The attitude you take can be affected by what you say. If everyday a student came to school and said, "I can't do it," at some point, the student might start to believe it! How a student feels about him or herself can be affected by their words!

5. Distribute to the class the Self-Talk reproducible.
   a. The students will decide which sayings are negative and which are positive and then place the negative statements in the trash can and the positive statements into the mind.
   b. Discuss how the students identified which self-talk sayings should go in their mind and which should be in the trash.

6. Distribute the Self-Talk Assessment.

Data

Quantitative: 90% of the students will be able to identify thoughts that are negative and positive; the students will be able to recognize that their self-talk can affect their sense of self.

Answers for the Self-Talk Assessment:

1. A
2. B
3. C
4. E

Total points for assessment: 4

Optional Lesson Extensions

(adding five to ten minutes to a lesson)

1. **Real World Buckets**—When using the bucket, use a third volunteer to indicate that most people have some negative and some positive self-talk comments.
2. **Lighten Up**—Using the bucket, show what happens when one person starts to change their attitude—starting out with a mind full of negative self-talk and then replacing those negative statements with positive ones. Discussion Questions:
   a. How could you tell the person's attitude was changing?
   b. What do you think happened to the student in school when their attitude changed?
   c. How might this person feel about their new perspective?

Name: ______________________ **Date:** ______________

Self-Talk Assessment

1. **How does positive self-talk help students learn?**
   a. Through encouraging students to keep on trying
   b. Through making students feel bad about their failures
   c. Through giving students all the answers magically
   d. Through exciting students into thinking that everything is okay
   e. None of the above

2. **Which phrase is considered positive self-talk?**
   a. "I can't do it, I'm going to the bathroom to hide"
   b. "I've never done this before, but I've figured out hard stuff before"
   c. "I'm going to try once, but then do something else if it does not make sense"
   d. "There is no way I can finish this! I need someone to give me the answers"
   e. All of the above

3. **How can negative self-talk be harmful?**
   a. It can be fun to talk negatively about yourself
   b. It can be encouraging to make fun of yourself
   c. It can be convincing and you may believe every negative thing you say
   d. It can be helpful to turn your day around
   e. None of the above

4. **What are the benefits of positive self-talk?**
   a. Becoming mentally strong, even when things are difficult
   b. Challenging yourself to learn new things
   c. Staying positive, even if things don't turn out as expected
   d. Finding new ways to see the good side of things
   e. All of the above

Name: ______________________________ Date: ______________

Self-Talk Reproducible

Directions: Where will you put these thoughts? Draw a line from the self-talk thought to where it needs to go.

	**I can never get this done, I'm not smart enough**	
	I'm such a loser	
	I'm sure I'll improve if I try harder	
	I know that I can finish this work	
	I hate myself	
	I think I can	
	What's the point, I never learn	
	If I don't know, I can find someone to help me	
	If I don't know, I'll never figure it out	
	I'm proud of what I can do	

Section Two:

Personal/Social Domain

The Steps Toward Happiness

Overview

Students will learn how to distinguish between the feelings of personal accomplishment and receiving gifts.

ASCA Standards

- PS.A1.2: Identify value, attitudes, and beliefs
- AD.A3.1: *Take responsibility for their actions*

Materials

Accomplishment Assessment
Happy Steps Reproducible

Approximate Time: 30 minutes

Procedures

1. Explain to the students that they are going to identify what they think would make them happier. They are to raise their hand to indicate the choice they like the most:
   a. Your family gives you a big bowl of ice cream OR you learn how to make cookies.
   b. You learn how to juggle OR your teacher gives you a prize for nothing.
2. Ask: "How does it make you feel when a person gives you something? How does it make you feel when you accomplish something by yourself?"
3. Explain that during this lesson, the students are going to identify what they think is more valued: personal accomplishment or objects (like presents/gifts).
4. Ask: "Students, consider what you think makes you happier over a long period of time—new toys/presents/objects or gaining new skills and abilities?"

5. Photocopy and distribute the Happy Steps reproducible to each student.
    a. Explain to the students that they are to pick their four favorite "items" and then place them on the Happy Steps. The more you like the "item" the higher it will be on the steps.
    b. Then, after the students are done ranking, they are to decide whether the happiness from the item comes from "me" or "not me" (meaning it comes from another person).
6. When the students are finished, ask the following discussion questions:
    a. Which category, "Me" or "Not Me," did you have more of? Have students examine their Happy Steps reproducible.
    b. Which items on the list can you take responsibility for? Can you be responsible for what people give you? Potential responses:
        - Students can be responsible for effort/personal tasks like learning to play an instrument or becoming skilled at a sport.
        - Students are not responsible for whether or not they receive gifts or if their family goes on a holiday vacation.
    c. Why can we control some things that make us happy and why are some things that make us happy not in our control? Potential responses:
        - Students can decide how much effort they put into school, sports, or learning new skills—when a student is responsible for his or her effort, then the student can be happy for what they have done on their own.
        - Students who receive prizes or presents may feel happy, but if the happiness comes from the item, then they are placing their feelings on what someone else has done.
    d. How do you feel when you can do something on your own? How do you feel when someone gives you something? Is it the same kind of happiness? Why or why not? Take appropriate responses.
7. Following the discussion, distribute Accomplishment Assessment.

Data

Quantitative: The classroom will score an average of 90% in understanding the differences between gifts and accomplishments; they will be able to identify beliefs about the different feelings that come from reaching a goal or receiving a present.

Answers for the Accomplishment Assessment:

1. D
2. A
3. B
4. B
5. B

Totally points for assessment: 5

Optional Lesson Extensions

(adding five to ten minutes to a lesson)

1. **Peppermints!**—Bring peppermints to the class; ask them if they would like them as a present or if they would like to earn them through successful lesson participation. Discuss the difference.
2. **Word Find**—Distribute a word find activity. Before beginning, ask the students if they would like to know what picture they are going to make or if they would like to figure it out on their own. What is more rewarding?
3. **Itemize**—Have the students make two columns on a piece of paper, have them write all the reasons why they like getting a gift in one column and all the reasons they like accomplishing a goal in the other. Have the students place a check mark in the column they think has greater meaning to them.

Name: ______________________________ Date: ________________

Accomplishment Assessment

1. Which of the following is a gift?
- a. Going to a movie because you behaved all week in school
- b. Getting five dollars from your grandmother because you helped clean her home
- c. Receiving straight "A"s on your report card because you worked hard in school
- d. Getting a new game because your uncle thought you would like it
- e. None of the above

2. When I learn a new skill...
- a. I am proud because it takes hard work to gain new skills
- b. I am sad because I don't need to learn anything new
- c. I am happy because someone gave me the skill
- d. I am sad because I had to work really hard
- e. None of the above

3. I am happy when I receive a gift because...
- a. It is the only way to feel proud of myself
- b. It shows that someone cares about me
- c. My brother or sister did not get one
- d. It lets me show off
- e. None of the above

4. What sentence makes the most sense when you are given a gift?
- a. "I worked really hard to have this birthday"
- b. "Thank you, I am so happy that you got this for me"
- c. "You must not like me if you don't get me any presents"
- d. "I get to control what I am given; I knew you would get this for me"
- e. None of the above

5. What sentence makes the most sense when you accomplish a task?
- a. "Thank you for giving me this accomplishment"
- b. "It took hard work, but I feel happy for reaching this goal"
- c. "You gave me this skill, thank you"
- d. "I'll never reach my goals if you don't give me a present"
- e. None of the above

Name: ______________________________ Date: ______________

Happy Steps

Directions: What will make you the happiest? Put your four favorite on the steps.

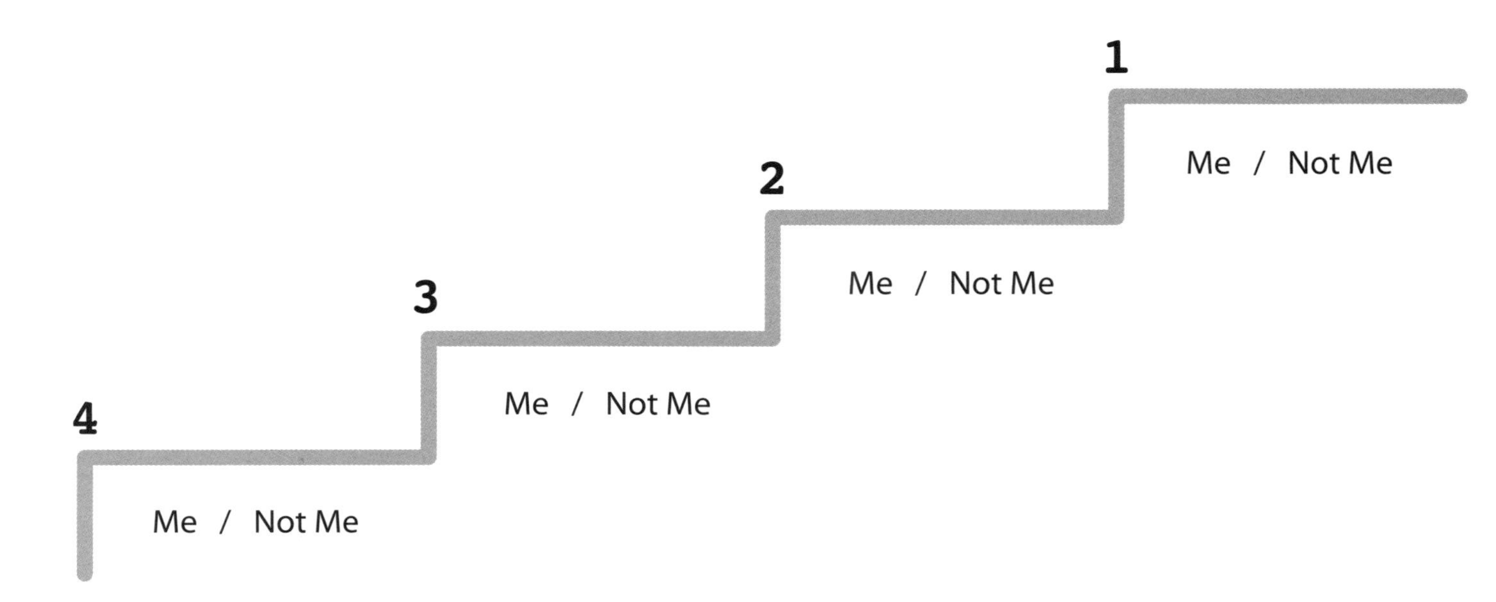

Make an "A" on a math test
Get a present
Playing music
Going to eat with your family
Writing a cool story
Knowing all the words on a spelling test
Your grandmother buying you a gift

Getting along with friends
Watching television
Going to Disney World with your family
Playing a sport really well
Making a new friend
Reading a book at a new level
A friend's dad takes you to the movies

All Hands. . .

Overview

Students will learn the importance of respecting different points-of-view and different ability levels.

ASCA Standards

- PS.A2.2: Respect alternative points of view
- PS.A2.3: Recognize, respect, and appreciate individual differences

Materials

Perspective Reproducible
Perspective Assessment
Writing Board

Approximate Time: 30 minutes

Procedures

1. Ask for two volunteers to assist in a competition:
   a. Each student will have to write the 26 letters of the alphabet on the board, but one student must use their non-dominant hand and the other must use their dominant hand.
   b. Ask the students to pay attention to who finishes first and who has better handwriting.
2. Pose the question: Would it be fair to say that [the student using their dominant hand] has neater, faster penmanship?
3. Take two more participants:
   a. Ask the student to draw a square; inside the square ask them to draw a circle; inside the circle ask them to draw a square. For the other student, ask the same, except he/she must complete the task with his/her eyes closed.
   b. Discuss whose geometric forms are most representative of the task.

4. Pose the question: Would it be fair to say that [the student who could draw with their eyes open] is a more accurate, more perceptive artist?

5. Explain: Everyone has different levels of abilities, no person is the same.
   a. Why is it important to recognize that everyone has different abilities?
   b. Why is it important to see that everyone looks at something a little bit differently? Potential answers:
      - For some, when they see a math problem, they are excited because they love math; for others they get worried because they don't think math is easy. Not everyone will like the same things.
      - Students can show respect by understanding that everyone will look at the world differently and knowing that all students have different abilities.
         1. Students can give positive comments to their classmates when the classmates challenge him or herself.
         2. Students can support each other through helping other students that need a little assistance.

6. Distribute the Perspective Reproducible—the students are to work in pairs.
   a. Discussion questions:
      - Did each of you draw the exact same thing? Most likely, they were different. Even if the students drew the same objects, they would look different.
      - Can you tell which of yours was "right?" Potential answers:
         1. Neither student was right because they were simply different.
         2. Both students were right because they drew what they believed to be the best or most difficult.

7. Distribute the Perspective Assessment.

Data

Quantitative: 90% of the students will be able to identify how respecting the differences in others' abilities is important to a positive classroom environment.

Answers to the Perspective Assessment:

1. C
2. B
3. E
4. C
5. D

Total points for assessment: 5

Optional Lesson Extensions

(adding five to ten minutes to a lesson)

1. ***The Blind Men and the Elephant*** by Karen Backstein and Annie Mitra, Scholastic Press—Read this story as an introduction to how people can be right about the same subject even though they all see it differently.
2. **Optical Illusions**—Use a set of optical illusions (Jar vs. Faces; Old Woman vs. Young Woman; Duck vs. Bunny) to discuss how often there is no right answer, but simply how something is perceived. These illusions are available in *201 Amazing Mind Bogglers* by Robert Bowman.
3. **$1,000,000**—Tell each student that they have to figure out how to spend a million dollars. After the students discuss how they would spend their money, discuss if any of the ways to spend the money was the "best" way.

Name: ____________________ **Date:** ____________

Perspective Assessment

1. **Which of the following is most CORRECT:**
   - a. Every student will be at the same level in all subjects
   - b. Students who struggle with one subject will be bad at all subjects
   - c. Students have different abilities in different subjects
   - d. Every student should like the same subjects
   - e. All of the above
2. **Which statement shows respect for differences?**
   - a. "I can do what you can, except better"
   - b. "What you are good at is different than what I am good at, no one is better than anyone else"
   - c. "Being bad in math means that you will be bad at everything"
   - d. "We are good at different subjects, but only one of us can be the best"
   - e. All of the above
3. **How can differences in abilities be a positive thing?**
   - a. I feel good when others help me when I have a hard time
   - b. I feel good when I help others that are having a hard time
   - c. People who have different abilities can teach each other what they know
   - d. People who have different abilities can be good group members
   - e. All of the above
4. **How can different opinions lead to more learning?**
   - a. By seeing how other people's opinions are wrong
   - b. By seeing how only one way is the best, and then to learn how to do it that way
   - c. By seeing different sides of the story, this gives more understanding of differences
   - d. By seeing different sides of the story, this lets people see what is right, once and for all
   - e. All of the above
5. **How can you prove to a friend that hamburgers are better than pizza?**
   - a. You can make your friend eat hamburgers everyday
   - b. You can't prove it because pizza is better than hamburgers
   - c. You can make your friend a list of reasons why hamburgers are better than pizza
   - d. You can't prove it because it is a personal perspective
   - e. All of the above

Name: ______________________________ Date: ________________

Perspective Reproducible

Directions: With a partner, complete the following drawings, compare what you did, and then answer the questions.

Draw the coolest animal that you can think of:	Write down AND solve the most complicated math problem that you can think of:

1. Can you tell if you or the other person was "more correct" for what was the coolest or most complicated?

2. What can you say to someone who has an opinion different from your own?

____

Draw a picture of a house, a tree, and a dog:	Draw a picture of a fast moving vehicle:

3. Find a compliment that describes a way that your partners drawings are different from your own; write it below:

____

4. Why is it important to appreciate other people's point-of-view?

____

CONFLICT!!!

Overview

Students will use a solution-focused strategy to learn how to solve conflicts.

ASCA Standards

- PS.B1.1: *Use a decision-making and problem-solving model*
- PS.B1.2: *Understand the consequences of decisions and choices*
- PS.B1.3: *Identify alternate solutions to a problem*
- PS.B1.6: *Know how to apply conflict resolution skills*

Materials

Solution Focused Graphic Organizer
Conflict Cards
Conflict Assessment

Approximate Time: 45 minutes

Procedures

1. Assign the students to tables; each table will have one conflict card that they will have to work together to solve.
   a. Explain to the students that rather than focusing on the problem, they will be focusing on the SOLUTIONS. They will use the Solution-Focused method of staying positive.
   b. Instead of just looking at the problems, the teams are to look for solutions.
2. By using the Solution-Focused Graphic Organizer, they will find multiple solutions to the conflict and then decide which solutions will be worth attempting first, second, then third.

3. When the students have come up with their three solutions, have each of the tables read their conflicts.
   a. The group will then read their solutions to the class.
   b. Allow the class to try to guess which solution the group picked; when the students are done guessing, have the group share their solutions and the order in which they placed them.
4. The following discussion questions are appropriate throughout the lesson:
   a. What does it feel like to come to a peaceful solution? Potential answers: Great, satisfying, makes me feel grown up, etc.
   b. How do you know when a conflict has been resolved? Potential answers: The problem is a little better, the problem goes away, people are friends again, etc.
   c. Sometimes the person who starts the conflict will do nothing to resolve it. How does it feel to do all the "work?" Potential answers: Frustrating, unfair, not nice, etc.
   d. Why do some people ignore their conflicts? Potential answers: They think they will go away by themselves, they don't know what to do, they don't think they need to help resolve it, etc.
   e. Why is it helpful to examine our past successes when dealing with present day conflicts? Potential answers: To see if a problem like this has been solved before, to find out how a person was already successful, to see that people can solve problems, etc.
5. Distribute the Conflict Resolution Assessment.

Data

Quantitative: 90% of the students will be able to identify the Solution Focused Method toward solving conflicts.

Answers for the Conflict Resolution Assessment:

1. B
2. C
3. A
4. A
5. D

Total points for assessment: 5

Name: ______________________________ Date: ________________

Conflict Resolution Assessment

1. **Another way to describe conflict resolution is:**
   a. Creating Problems
   b. Problem Solving
   c. Problem Starting
   d. Problem Ignoring
   e. None of the above
2. **If you have a conflict, what choice do you think is best?**
   a. Complaining about the conflict with a friend
   b. Wait for the conflict to go away by itself
   c. Focusing on different solutions to the conflict
   d. Ask someone else to solve your conflict
   e. None of the above
3. **The strategy that we have discussed in class is called:**
   a. Solution Focused
   b. Problem Focused
   c. Action Focused
   d. Method Focused
   e. None of the above
4. **TRUE or FALSE—Every conflict has some type of resolution**
   a. True
   b. False
5. **Why is it important to consider more than one resolution to a conflict?**
   a. Because the first resolution may not work
   b. Because it helps to keep the solution in focus and not the problem
   c. Because there are many solutions to one problem
   d. All of the above
   e. None of the above

Name: ______________________________ Date: ______________

Solution Focused Graphic Organizer:

Directions: Using the Conflict Cards, come up with three possible solutions to the conflict and then decide which solution you would try first, second, and then third! Finish by answering the discussion questions.

Summarize the Conflict (1 sentence or less)		
What I think I can do to resolve the conflict…	What I think I can do to resolve the conflict…	What I think I can do to resolve the conflict…
I rate this solution **1st** **2nd** **3rd**	I rate this solution **1st** **2nd** **3rd**	I rate this solution **1st** **2nd** **3rd**

Why do you think your first place solution will work best?

____

Why will your second place solution work?

____

Why will your third place solution work?

____

Conflict Cards:

Directions: Cut and distribute one conflict to each group of students. They are to use the Solution Focused Graphic Organizers to come up with three possible solutions to the conflicts.

At home—you and your sister want to watch two different television shows that are on at the same time. Both of you start pulling on the remote so you can control the television.

At school—you are mad at another student because he told everyone at his table your grade on your last math test. You had a hard time on the math test and wanted your grades to be kept private.

At home—you live with your grandmother, mother, and little brother. You feel all alone because it seems like your brother gets all of the attention in the family.

At school—several students are picking on you because you haven't had a new pair of shoes for a long time because your family is struggling with money.

At home—some of the kids in your neighborhood never do their homework and they are always outside playing games. The minute you start doing your homework, they want you to go outside and play.

At school—you and another student get the best grades in the class. As a result, you become very competitive with her and always want to be better then her. You always get angry at her when she does well on an assignment. Whenever she talks to you, you are very rude to her.

Fair Play and Play Fair

Overview

Students will learn the importance of following rules and how that creates a sense of fairness.

ASCA Standards

- PS.C1.2: Learn about the relationship between rules, laws, safety and the protection of rights as an individual
- PS.A1.9: *Demonstrate cooperative behavior in groups*
- PS.A2.6: *Use effective communications skills*

Materials

Game Description Form
Fair Play Assessment

Approximate Time: 30 Minutes

Procedures

1. Place the students in groups of four or five.
2. Ask the students, "What would happen if you were playing a board game that didn't have any rules?"
   a. Take appropriate responses and then state, "If we didn't have rules, then people may get confused as to what they are supposed to do. Maybe no one could tell who won. Rules allow us to make sense of what is supposed to happen."
3. Ask, "What would happen if there were no rules for people who were driving around on the street?"
   a. Take appropriate responses and then state, "If it weren't for rules, which are also called laws, then people could get hurt. It would be difficult to go places because everyone might be racing around and there would be no order."

4. Ask, "So what would happen if half the people knew the rules and the other half did not know them?"
   a. Indicate, "This could be very confusing. Some people might think that it's not fair; others might think that people are cheating. It's important for everyone to work together as a group."

5. Distribute the Game Description Form to the groups. Explain that they are going to play a "rule-making" game. To play:
   a. At the table, you will have to come up with all the rules that you can think of that will make the game fair. The more descriptive your rules, the more others will be able to play the game.
   b. You are not allowed to say the name of the game in your rules.
   c. When everyone is done with their Game Description Form, the groups will share their rules with the rest of the class. See if the other groups can guess the name of your game!

6. When complete, ask the following discussion questions:
   a. Was it important to have descriptive rules? Why?
   b. Why is it important for everyone to know the rules of the game?
   c. When playing a game, how can you make sure it is the most fair for everyone playing?
   d. If you don't know how to play, what are some strategies you could try so you could play fairly?
      - Read the rules.
      - Watch people play until figuring out what to do.

7. Distribute the Fair Play Assessment.

Data

Quantitative: 90% of students will be able to identify the importance of following rules.

Answers for the Fair Play Assessment:

1. D
2. B
3. D
4. D
5. B

Total points for assessment: 5

Optional Lesson Extensions

(adding five to ten minutes to a lesson)

1. At the beginning of the lesson, walk into the room and without saying a word draw a tic-tac-toe board on the board. Invite someone up to play, but do not talk. As the game progresses, make a move that is not normally allowed. When the class indicates cheating, let them know that no one spoke about the rules of the game.
   a. What would have helped before the game began?
   b. Why are rules important to playing a game?
2. Take the class outside to play "Red Light, Green Light." Before going outside, on a piece of paper give half of the class the rules that say "Go on Red, Stop on Green" and the other half of the class has the rules "Go on Green, Stop on Red." At the conclusion of the game:
   a. Who won?
   b. Who followed the rules?
   c. Why was there confusion?
   d. What would happen if in real life, half the people thought you had to stop at green lights and the other half thought you had to stop on red lights?

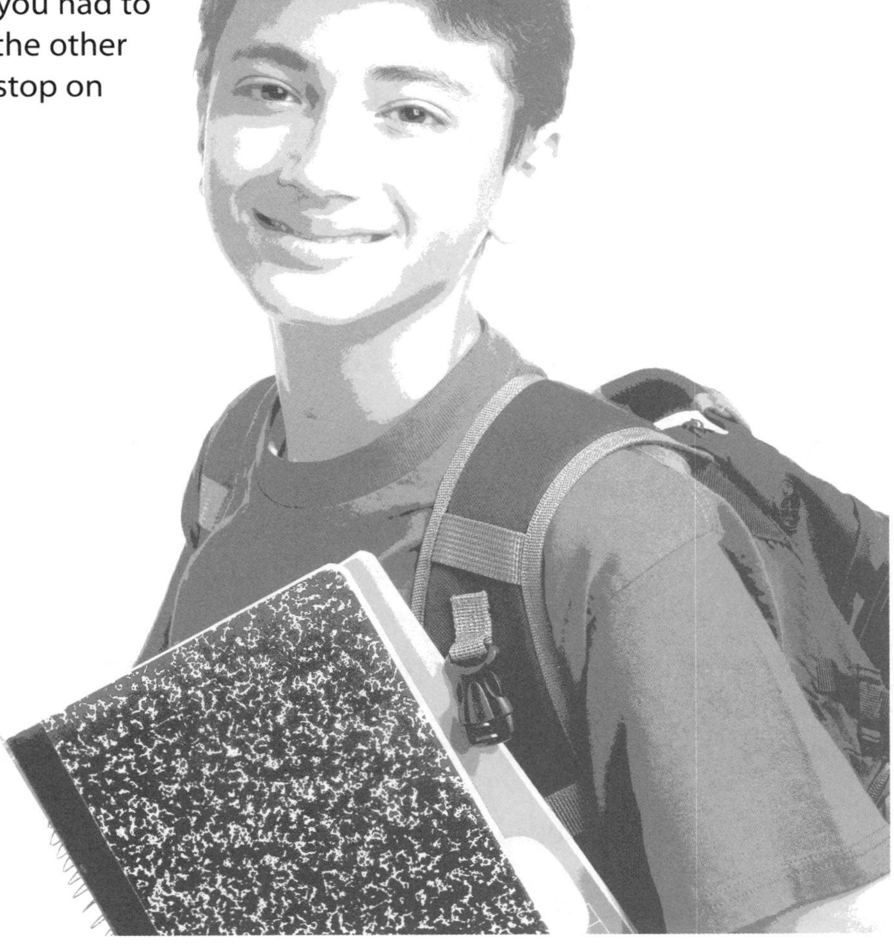

Name: ______________________ Date: ____________

Fair Play Assessment

1. **What reason (s) do people have rules and laws?**
   a. To keep people safe
   b. To make things fair
   c. To make sure that people know what to do
   d. To show people how to treat others with respect
   e. All of the Above
2. **How can you make sure that people play fairly?**
   a. Make sure that only one person knows the rules
   b. Make sure that everyone knows how to play
   c. Make sure that if someone does not know the rules, they get in trouble
   d. Make sure that cheating is okay
   e. All of the above
3. **You and a friend play a board game in two different ways. What should you do?**
   a. Play the game by both rules at the same time
   b. Don't play the game at all
   c. Figure out whose rules are better
   d. Decide on the rules before starting to play
   e. All of the above
4. **You are deciding on rules to a board game. Which is NOT fair and should NOT be used?**
   a. After you roll the dice, pass them to your left
   b. If you land on the red square, go back to the start
   c. If you land on the green square, move three spaces forward
   d. If you are a boy, you get your turn skipped
   e. All of the above
5. **A rule for the cafeteria states: Girls always get to sit down first and wherever they want. This is;**
   a. A good rule because it is fair
   b. A bad rule because it is unfair
   c. A good rule because everyone can follow it
   d. A bad rule because everyone does not know it
   e. None of the above

Game Description Forms

Cut and distribute to the groups.

Instructions: In groups, create the rules to these games. Do not say the name of the game in the rules!

Duck, Duck Goose

1.

2.

3.

4.

5.

Checkers

1.

2.

3.

4.

5.

Tag

1.

2.

3.

4.

5.

Hide and Go Seek

1.

2.

3.

4.

5.

Get Help . . . Be Help

Overview

Students will learn to use different members of their community as a resource for assistance.

ASCA Standards

- PS.C1.5: Differentiate between situations requiring peer support and situations requiring adult professional help
- PS.C1.6: Identify resource people in the school and community, and know how to seek their help

Materials

Resources Assessment
Problem-Identification Scale

Approximate Time: 30 minutes

Procedures

1. Explain to the students that some issues can be handled by themselves and other issues require more help. It is important to be able to differentiate between situations that can be handled by one's self and situations that require help from parents, teachers, or other resources in the community.
2. Ask the students to name situations—attempt to identify the varying degrees of assistance needed, for example:

Situation	Resource
Seeing someone steal something in a store	A police officer or the store manager
Having a huge project to do	A friend who can help out, a parent, teacher
An argument with a sibling	Myself
Bullying in the classroom	Myself, the counselor, a teacher, a trusted adult

3. Distribute the Problem-Identification Scale to each student. The students are to identify the level of concern and which resource they would use to attain help.
4. Discussion questions:
   a. Why is it important to know the difference between issues that can be handled by yourself and issues that need adult assistance?
   b. What would happen if you went to an adult with every concern?
   c. What would happen if you never went to adults with concerns?
5. Conclude by distributing the Resources Assessment.

Data

Quantitative: 90% of the students will be able to identify the appropriate resource depending on the situation.

Student-Centric: Using the Problem-Solving Scale, data can be gathered on student's perceptions of what may be major stressors for themselves.

Answers for the Resources Assessment:

1. C
2. D
3. A
4. C
5. A

Total points for assessment: 5

Optional Lesson Extensions

(adding five to ten minutes to a lesson)

1. **Know the Roles**—Discuss with the students the various responsibilities of members in the community. How do different members of the community assist people? When is it appropriate to call Animal Control? What is the job of Social Services?
2. **Further Peer Support**—Talk with the students about how to give appropriate support to their peers. How can they support their peers academically, emotionally, or socially? Also discuss ways that some students give "support," but in reality is not helpful:
   a. Sharing homework with peers
   b. Hiding harmful secrets for a peer
   c. "Covering" for a peer; a method of enabling

Name: ______________________ Date: ______________

Resources Assessment

1. **What is the first question you should ask yourself when there is a concern?**
   a. "Who is going to help me"
   b. "How am I going to do this all by myself"
   c. "Is this a problem that I can take care of or do I need someone else"
   d. "Will anyone help me if I try to get some help"
   e. All of the above
2. **Why is it important to recognize how serious (or not serious) an issue is?**
   a. To figure out if it is something that you can do on your own
   b. To figure out if you need to stay away and leave it alone
   c. To figure out what kind of resources will be needed
   d. To figure out if the problem needs immediate attention or can be solved later
   e. All of the above
3. **You see a student in your class copy off of someone else's paper. Which resource will be the FIRST place to go for help?**
   a. The teacher
   b. The principal
   c. The counselor
   d. The police officer
   e. All of the above
4. **You see a person you don't recognize walking around the outside of the school grounds. What would be the safest course of action to take?**
   a. Go up and see who the person is
   b. Tell all of your friends where to find the person
   c. Tell one of the teachers that you see a strange person
   d. Tell no one, because it isn't that serious of a concern
   e. All of the above
5. **What is important about finding the appropriate resource to help with problems, issues, and concerns?**
   a. The appropriate resource handles the problem in the best way possible
   b. Finding the right resource shows people how responsible I can be
   c. Others will feel good about being able to help out a friend
   d. The situation will disappear and never show up again
   e. All of the above

Name: ______________________ Date: ______________

Problem-Identification Scale

Directions: Rate the level of seriousness for each of the concerns. Then, also decide whether you need to work on the concern yourself, with a peer (a classmate), a teacher, your family, or a member of the community (police officer, firefighter, etc.)

How serious is the concern? (1 is not serious at all and 5 is very serious)

1 ⟵⟶ 5

Who should help?

Myself, a classmate, a teacher, my family, or a community member—write all sources that apply.

1. **You get into an argument with your friend over who is better at baseball.**

   How serious? ______________________

   Who is your resource? ______________________

2. **You see a strange adult walking around outside the front of your home—this person begins looking in windows.**

   How serious? ______________________

   Who is your resource? ______________________

3. **You get your report card with an "F" in history.**

   How serious? ______________________

   Who is your resource? ______________________

4. **While at home you are helping cook dinner and you accidentally touch the stove.**

   How serious? ______________________

   Who is your resource? ______________________

5. **You want to set up a football game after school and need help organizing.**

   How serious? ______________________

   Who is your resource? ______________________

I'm Like You (and Sometimes I'm Not)

Overview

Students will learn ways that they are alike and different from their classmates; they will learn how to connect with one another, even if they are different.

ASCA Standards

- PS.A2.2: Respect alternative points of view
- PS.A2.3: Recognize, accept, respect and appreciate individual differences

Materials

Individual Differences Assessment
"What I like" Worksheet

Approximate Time: 45 minutes

Procedures

1. Begin by stating, "No one is exactly alike. We know that no two people are exactly the same, but what does that mean?" Take appropriate responses.
2. Ask, "So if we know that we are all different, how can we find out our similarities?" Some students may talk about looking at each others' clothes or finding out about people's age, and some may bring up the fact that they need to talk to one another.
3. Explain, "One of the best ways to get to know people is to find out what they like and see if you have similar interests."
4. Distribute the "What I like" worksheet.
   a. In the middle star, they are to put their name.

b. In the circle, they are to write a list of all the things that they think are interesting or cool.
- This could be video games or soccer or comic books or horseback riding.

5. When the class has completed their worksheets, they are to see how people are connected.
a. Tell the students to leave their worksheets at their seats.
b. Students are then to walk around the room and look at everyone's worksheet.
- They then write their name inside the square and draw a line from their name to two different interests that they would consider their favorite, too.
- If the students have written down the exact same things, then they are to circle those things.

At the conclusion, the worksheet should look similar to the following example:

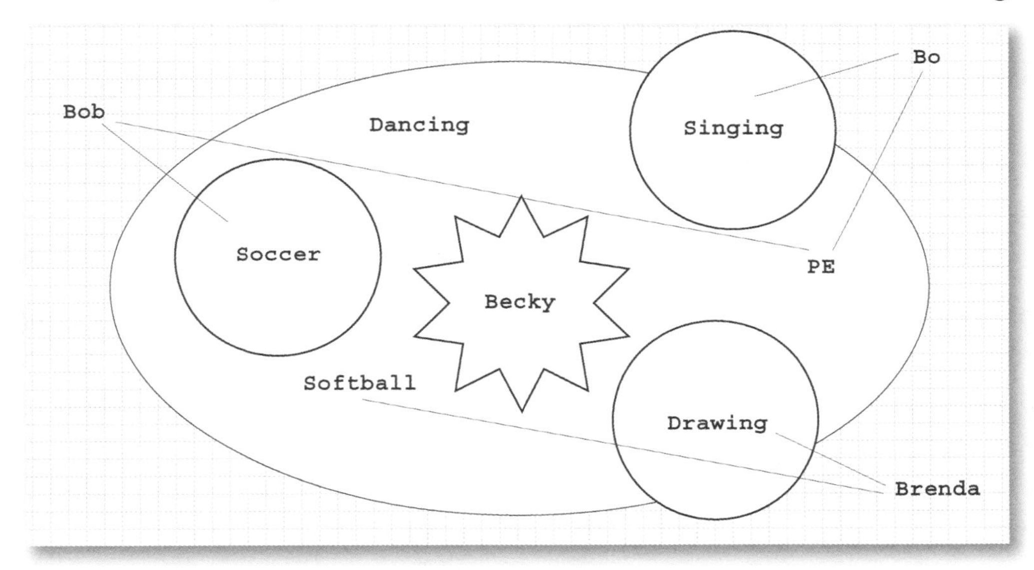

In the example, Becky likes dancing, singing, soccer, softball, and drawing. Bob also likes P.E. and soccer. He also wrote "soccer" on his worksheet, so he circled it on Becky's form. Bo likes P.E. and singing. He wrote singing on his form, so he circled it on Becky's. Brenda likes softball and drawing. She wrote down drawing on her form too, so she circled it on Becky's sheet.

6. After the students have finished (or after 5-10 minutes), ask the following discussion questions:
a. Who can name one person they have a connection with?
b. Who can name one person who they have a difference with?
c. How can you use this worksheet as a conversation starter?
d. How does it feel to know that people are different than you?
e. How can you connect with people who are different than you?

7. Conclude the lesson and distribute the Individual Differences Assessment.

Data

Quantitative: 90% of the students will be able to identify how they are similar and alike with students in the classroom; students will be able to indicate ways to show respect for people with differences.

Answers for the Individual Differences Assessment:

1. C
2. B
3. B
4. D

Total points for assessment: 4

Optional Lesson Extensions

(adding five to ten minutes to a lesson)

1. **Classroom Connection**—Have the students create a classroom list of interests; these can be used as connection topics throughout the school year.
2. **Individuality Observation**—Have the students play a game of "Find the most different." They are to go around the room and see how many topics they have that are not the same as other students.
3. **Total Connection**—Similarly, see if the students can find a topic to which everyone has a connection.

Name: ______________________________ Date: ______________

Individual Differences Assessment

1. **What is helpful in learning about other students' interests?**
   a. Talking about yourself
   b. Staying quiet until the students talk to you
   c. Asking students questions about their interests
   d. Hiding from students that want to talk to you
   e. None of the above
2. **Which question would help you learn about another student?**
   a. "Want to hear about my favorite game"
   b. "What is your favorite movie"
   c. "I can't wait to go home and play"
   d. "Want to hear a secret"
   e. None of the above
3. **Two students have different interests. What will help them understand each other?**
   a. Nothing. The students are too different
   b. The student can try to learn why they like different things
   c. The two students can stay away from each other
   d. One student can force the other student to be like them
   e. None of the above
4. **Which statement do you think is the most appropriate?**
   a. "People who are interested in different subjects will never get along"
   b. "For people to get along, they need to have the same interest in all of the same subjects"
   c. "People who are different than I am need to like what I like to be friends"
   d. "For people to get along, it helps to try to learn about how we are alike and different"
   e. None of the above

Name: ______________________ Date: ______________

Individual Differences Graphic Organizer

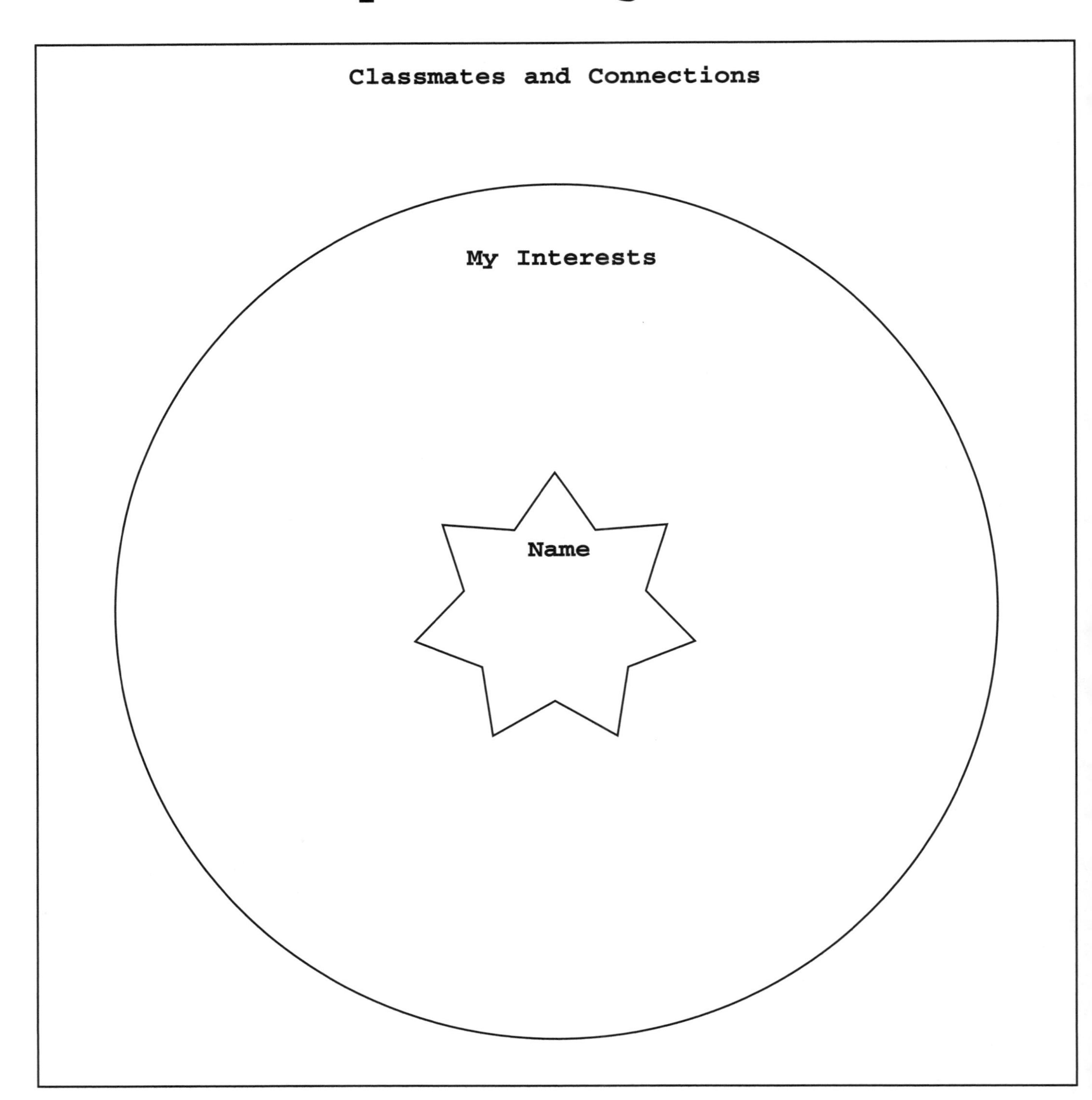

The Way I Make it Through My Day

Overview

Students will recognize how to turn their day around after a negative event occurs. They will develop strategies for overcoming daily challenges.

ASCA Standards

- PS.B1.3: Identify alternative solutions to a problem
- PS.B1.4: Develop effective coping skills for dealing with problems

Materials

"My Day in a Maze" worksheet
Overcoming Challenges Assessment

Approximate Time: 30 minutes

Procedures

1. Ask the students questions pertaining to events going from bad to worse. (i.e., "Let's say you are in a car and you run out of gas. Would you then let all the air out of the tires? If you stubbed your toe on a brick, would you then bonk your head against a tree?")
2. Explain that in school, it is very common to make choices that lead from bad to worse. Ask: "Have you ever been in a little bit of trouble in the morning and it felt like your whole day was ruined?" Let the class share examples of times where one event created a problem that persisted for the whole day.
3. Let the students know that this does not always have to be that way—they can make a choice of how they want their day to turn out. Just because one event happens that they didn't like doesn't mean that the whole day is going to be awful.

4. Here are some examples of events that can ruin your day, if you choose:
   a. Getting to school late and not knowing what to do on an assignment
   b. Forgetting your homework
   c. Getting in trouble for talking in the hallway
5. Ask the students if they can think of other general examples of events that can be a problem during the school day.
6. Present the following scenarios and ask the students what they could choose to do to make the situation go from bad to worse AND what they could do to make the situation go from bad to better:
   a. You and a friend get into an argument at lunch.
   b. You raise your hand to answer a question and don't get called on.
   c. You trip during science and break a beaker.
7. With each situation, let the students know that there is a choice about what action can be taken—ask the students what they could say to themselves to prompt them to turn their day around. **Students can choose to make their day better or make their day worse.**
8. Distribute the "My Day in a Maze" reproducible. Explain to the students that they need to get through the maze, but just like a day, there are all sorts of problems that cause students to get stuck. When a student runs into the letter (A, B, C, or D), they must go to the corresponding question and write a sentence about what they would do to not let that event ruin their day.
9. After the activity, discuss with the students what actions they took to help their day.
10. Conclude the lesson by distributing the Overcoming Challenges Assessment.

Data

Quantitative: 90% of the students will be able to identify strategies that can help them improve their day.

Answers for the Overcoming Challenges Assessment:

1. B
2. C
3. C
4. D
5. A

Total points for assessment: 5

Reading Extensions

The Very Angry Day that Amy Didn't Have by Lawrence E. Shapiro

My Mouth is a Volcano by Julia Cook

Optional Lesson Extensions

(adding five to ten minutes to a lesson)

1. Have the students role-play the scenarios with two conclusions—one in which the students take their days from bad to worse. The other where the students take their days from bad to okay.
2. Ask the students to share their "worst school day" ever. Prompt them to find the places in the day that they could have turned their day around. Some discussion questions:
   a. Was any part of the day based on a decision you made?
   b. What other choices could have been made to help the day get better?
   c. At what point did you realize that you could have made better decisions?
3. Have the students draw a picture of someone making a bad decision. Then pass the picture to a classmate and see if they can identify what the decision is and what the better decision would be—have that student draw a picture on the other side of a successful decision with the same situation.

Name: ______________________ Date: ______________

Overcoming Challenges Assessment

1. **You want to go to the classroom prize box, but you know that if you behave inappropriately one more time, then you will receive no reward AND you will get a conduct report sent home. What could you say to yourself to turn your day around?**
   a. "I'm never going to get a prize; I don't care what I do"
   b. "I'm not going to get what I want if I keep behaving poorly"
   c. "I know my teacher will never let me get there, she hates me"
   d. "I'm the only one who gets in trouble in this classroom, it's not fair"
   e. None of the above

2. **You get off the school bus in the morning, and just as you are about to walk into school, you fall into a puddle of water. What choice is BEST to keep you from ruining your day?**
   a. Throw your book bag down and yell at the bus driver
   b. Push your friend who laughed at you for falling
   c. Go to the restroom and dry yourself off
   d. Run home from school and stay there until you feel better
   e. None of the above

3. **You get a quiz back and you missed almost all of the questions. What choice is BEST to keep you from ruining your day?**
   a. Rip up your quiz
   b. Tell your teacher that you have to make a good grade
   c. Ask your teacher if you can try it again
   d. Bang your head on the desk
   e. None of the above

4. **You forgot to do your homework assignment! Which solution WILL NOT help your day get better?**
   a. Ask the teacher if you can do the assignment during recess or free time
   b. Ask the teacher if you can go home and do the assignment and turn it in for a late grade
   c. See if there is extra credit that you can do during the day to make up for the lost points from the homework
   d. Ask a friend to give you the answers so you can turn in the assignment on time
   e. All of the answers will help make your day better

5. **When something bad happens at school...**
   a. You can choose if it will make your day bad
   b. Your day will be bad no matter what
   c. Your behavior has no effect on how your day will be
   d. Your day will be good if you keep making bad choices
   e. None of the above

Name: ______________________ Date: ______________

My Day in a Maze

Directions: When you run into one of the letters, you are stuck! Write a sentence about what you will do to solve the problem so you can keep on moving!

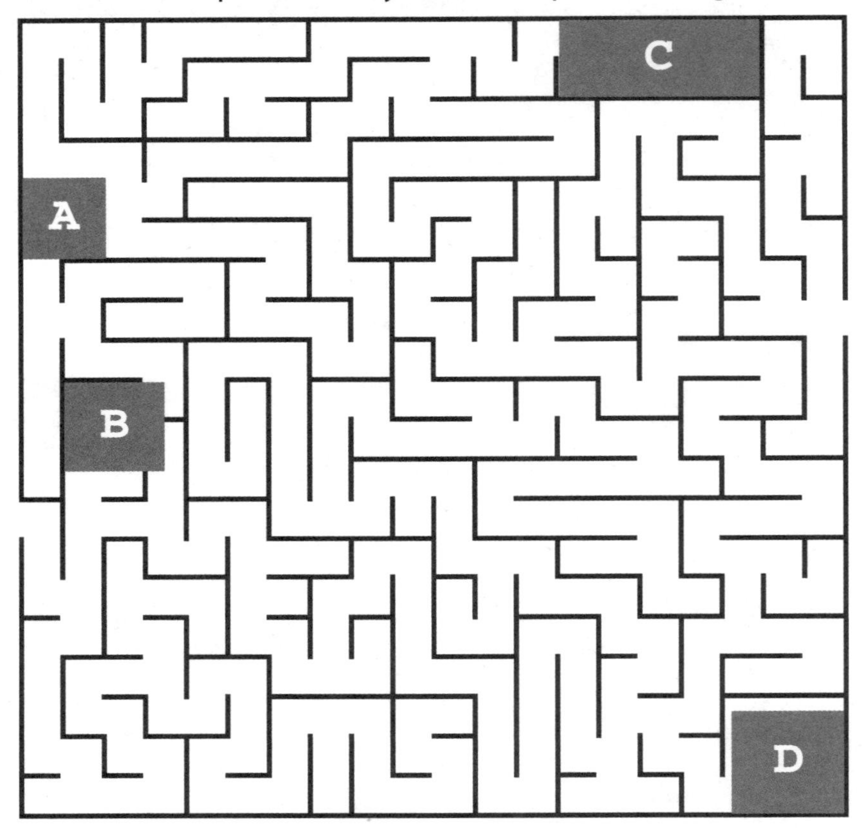

A. You and a friend are talking during an assignment and have no idea what to do. How do you get back on track?

____

B. You are in a bad mood and yelled at someone in the class. How do you get unstuck?

____

C. You don't want to read today, so you put your head down on your desk and ignore the teacher. What can you do?

____

D. On the bus you got written up for jumping around and now you have to see the principal. What can you do to turn your day around?

____

Sorry is Not Enough

Overview

Students will learn an effective method for apologizing and how an appropriate apology can alleviate conflict.

ASCA Standards

- PS.A2.6: Use affective communication skills
- PS.B1.6: Know how to apply conflict resolution skills

Materials

Apology Assessment
Apology Steps
Apology Reproducible

Approximate Time: 30 minutes

Procedures

1. Ask the students to explain how some kids will give an apology but they don't mean it. How can you tell? Some possible answers:
   a. The tone of voice is sarcastic or negative.
   b. Behaviors between people do not improve.
   c. Eye contact is not made.
2. Explain to the students that if the goal of an apology is to make a situation better, then the word "Sorry" is not enough. Behaviors and actions will have to change to make a difference!
3. Display the Apology Sheet. Explain that one strategy toward giving an appropriate apology takes three steps:
   a. Part 1: Say, "I'm sorry for [name the reason]" with sincerity and eye contact.

b. Part 2: Say, "I know it is my fault" to show ownership of the conflict.
c. Part 3: Say, "What can I do to make things different?" This shows an effort to make a change.

4. Pair off classmates and have them role play giving an apology using this strategy. The students can make up any scenario they want to practice. Some examples:
   a. One brother pushes another brother because he took the last soda.
   b. Students in class pick on each other and cause hurt feelings.
   c. One kid uses up the whole computer time without thinking about the other student.
5. Let students share their apology strategy.
6. Distribute the Apology Reproducible; if the students wish to share these they can, but it is also understandable if they would like to keep them private.
7. Discussion questions:
   a. What does a true, honest apology do for people in conflict?
   b. How can giving an apology make you feel better?
   c. Does giving a sincere apology show responsibility? How?
   d. Why is it important for a person's behavior and actions to be different for an apology to make a situation better?
8. Distribute the Apology Assessment.

Data

Quantitative: 90% of the students will be able to identify how to give a sincere apology, why doing so shows responsibility, and why it can make a difference in a conflict.

Student-Centric: Students can use their Apology Reproducible as a stepping stone to discuss a conflict they are having with another person. Follow up with students who indicated that they would use this strategy—investigate whether or not it made a difference for them.

Answers for the Apology Assessment:

1. I'm sorry for..., I know it is my fault., What can I do to make things different? (3 points)
2. B
3. A
4. C
5. E

Total points for assessment: 7

Optional Lesson Extensions

(adding five to ten minutes to a lesson)

Who Has the Courage?—Discuss with the students that apologizing is sometimes the hardest thing to do because it takes humility and the ability to see that they are wrong. Discuss with the students their thoughts on whether they think apologizing shows courage or if it shows weakness. On the board, write down reasons why people may think that apologizing is a sign of weakness and how it can also be a sign of strength.

Name: ______________________ Date: ____________

Apology Assessment

1. **What are the three steps to giving an apology? Place an "X" in front of the three that are apologies.**

	Say, "I'm sorry if you are sorry."
	Say, "You know you made me mad and that's why I did what I did."
	Say, "What can I do to make things different?"
	Say, "I'm sorry, but it's not my fault."
	Say, "I'm sorry for..."
	Say, "I'll feel better after you leave me alone for a while."
	Say, "Just forget that I did anything, I was only teasing."
	Say, "I know it is my fault."

2. **What are the benefits of giving an appropriate apology?**
   a. The person will think that you are a chicken for apologizing
   b. You and the other person will feel better about making things better between the two of you
   c. You will now have the ability to make the other person feel bad for not apologizing to you
   d. The person you have a conflict with will probably become your best friend ever
   e. None of the above

3. **How does giving an appropriate apology show responsibility?**
   a. You are taking ownership of what you have done
   b. You are showing everyone how to give a good apology
   c. You are doing what it takes to stay out of trouble
   d. You are making sure that no one ever gets upset
   e. None of the above

4. **Which apology seems to be the most appropriate?**
   a. "FINE! I'm sorry! Whatever"
   b. Saying I'm sorry while your back is turned
   c. "I'm sorry for hurting your feelings. What can I do differently"
   d. "I'm only sorry because I got in trouble; he started it"
   e. None are appropriate

5. **How can you tell if your apology is appropriate?**
   a. You and the other person feel better about the conflict
   b. You feel good about taking responsibility for your actions
   c. You are no longer angry or the other person is no longer angry
   d. You have made a plan to make sure things will be okay in the future
   e. All of the above

Name: ______________________ Date: ______________

Apology Reproducible

Directions: Follow the steps to an appropriate apology! Will you be willing to give it a try?

Apology Steps

Step 1. I'm sorry.
When you say, "I'm sorry," you are letting the person know that something wrong has been done.

Step 2. I know it is my fault.
When you say, "I know it is my fault" you are taking responsibility for your actions. This is a big step! It takes courage to admit when you are wrong.

Step 3. What can I do to make it different?
When you ask, "What can I do to make it different?" you are showing that you want to make the effort to make things better.

1. Write down a problem you are having or maybe a problem you once had that has not been resolved.

   ____

   ____

2. Write down why an apology is necessary.

   ____

   ____

3. Write down how you could tell that you were wrong. What happened?

   ____

   ____

4. Write down what you are willing to do differently to make things better.

   ____

   ____

5. Are you willing to tell the person? If you are, when will you do it?

   ____

   ____

Did You Hear?

Overview

Students will recognize the negative effects of gossiping; students will be able to use verbal strategies to stop gossiping when they see it; they will learn how to protect friendships.

ASCA Standards

- PS.A1.7: Recognize personal boundaries, rights, and privacy needs
- PS.A2.8: Learn how to make and keep friends

Materials

Gossip Cards
Gossiping Quiz
Gossiping Assessment

Approximate Time: 30 minutes

Procedures

1. Place the class into two or three small groups.
2. Ask the class if they know the word for when people talk about each other in a negative way. Some might say "rumors" and others might say "gossip." Both answers are correct, but for this class period focus on the word gossip.
3. Explain to the class that gossip is a form of bullying. Ask the class, "How do you think that gossip is a form of bullying?"
   a. It can make people feel sad.
   b. Gossip may try to embarrass other kids.
   c. Some people do it to be mean.
   d. People who gossip are trying to hurt other kids' feelings.

4. After discussing the ties of Gossip to Bullying, explain to the students that when gossip spreads, it becomes worse and worse because whatever was said keeps changing.
5. The students will see an example of this by playing "gossip telephone" at their tables.
   a. One person at the table will have the Gossip Card. The student will read the card and then whisper to the next person what is on the card. The "gossip" will then be whispered around the circle. The last person will write on the board what they think they heard.
   b. Each group will do the same and then compare their answers to the initial "gossip card."
6. Discussion Questions:
   a. How can talking about other people cause confusion?
   b. Why can talking about other people cause feelings to get hurt?
   c. How would it feel if the gossip being spread was about you?
7. Offer the students the following suggestions as a way to stave off gossip from their lives:
   a. If a classmate is talking about another student in a negative way, let him or her know what the classmate is doing. Say, "What you are doing is gossip—I won't listen to it."
   b. Change the subject so that someone's feelings don't get hurt. Say, "Instead of talking about someone else, why don't you tell me about you?"
   c. You can also bring the other person into the picture (unless you think it might cause more problems). Say, "Listen, I don't like to talk about people who aren't around. Let me go see if they know what you are talking about."
8. Conclude the lesson by distributing the Gossip Assessment.

Data

Quantitative: 90% of the students will be able to identify how gossip is harmful to friendships. The students will recognize the importance of personal boundaries, needs, and rights.

Answers for the Gossip Assessment:

1. C
2. E
3. B
4. A
5. D

Total points for assessment: 5

Optional Reading and Website Extensions

1. *Queen Bees and Wannabes: Helping Your Daughter Survive Cliques, Gossip, Boyfriends, and Other Realities of Adolescence* by Rosalind Wiseman
2. *The Big Bad Rumor* by Jonathan Meres
3. *Say Something* by Peggy Moss and Lea Lyon
4. *Just Kidding* by Trudy Ludwig
5. *Alley Oops* by Janice Levy
6. *Please Stop. I Don't Like That!* by Sandy Ragona and Amy Tranel
7. http://pbskids.org/itsmylife/friends/rumors/index.html

Name: ______________________ Date: ______________

Gossiping Assessment

1. **Which of the following statements do you think is gossip?**
   a. My favorite movie is "High School Musical"
   b. Jennifer and I are good friends
   c. Marcos likes to watch baby cartoons when he goes home from school
   d. I think that last math test we took was hard
   e. All of the above

2. **What happens when kids talk about other classmates?**
   a. Information can get mixed up
   b. Kids can get their feelings hurt
   c. Someone might get angry about being talked about
   d. People can lose friends about something that is not true
   e. All of the above

3. **How can you get someone to stop gossiping about another person?**
   a. Say, "Tell me more, that's interesting"
   b. Say, "Gossip just causes problems. Let's talk about something else"
   c. Say, "Gosh, I can't wait to tell the rest of the class"
   d. Say, "Well, let me tell you about something I heard"
   e. All of the above

4. **How can you tell if a classmate is gossiping?**
   a. They are talking about someone who is not around to explain what is true and what is not
   b. They are talking about things they like and don't like
   c. They are talking about something they watched on television
   d. They are asking questions about a class assignment
   e. All of the above

5. **What is something else you can tell to someone to stop gossiping?**
   a. "I know you are gossiping, but that's okay"
   b. "Gossip is the best way to make friends"
   c. "I'd rather not talk to you at all than have you spread gossip"
   d. "Gossip is always true; I believe everything that everyone says"
   e. All of the above

Gossip Cards

Directions: Distribute one gossip card to each group.

Someone told me Tommy told Jonny to go to the store to pick up some cigarettes and give them to Sally.

I heard Keandra didn't go home last night because her mom and dad forgot to pick her up.

Someone told me that Steven copied off of Juan's test in Mrs. Phillips' room and he still failed the test.

I heard that Eddie and Trey got in an argument and Kelly told me that they are going to get into a fight after school on the playground.

Someone told me that Elizabeth and Simon's parents were going to get married and they were going to move to Egypt.

Name Your Price

Overview

Students will learn to identify the difference between long-term contentment and short-term contentment that changes. Students will see how some wants and desires change over time and how others remain constant

ASCA Standards

- PS.A1.2: Identify values, attitudes, and beliefs
- PS.A1.4: Understand that change is part of growth

Materials

Priority Assessment
Bidding Sheets
Bidding Tags
Play Money

Approximate Time: 30 to 45 minutes

Procedure

1. Ask the students to identify their favorite book when they were in first grade. Ask, "Is this book still your favorite book?" Discuss with students why their book interests have changed. Discuss with the students various "favorite, most important" aspects of their lives that changed as they got older:
   a. Favorite cartoons or television shows
   b. Favorite music
   c. Favorite sports
2. Indicate to the students that as people mature, what they see as important begins to change.

3. Explain that today they will identify what they think is important by playing an Auction Game. Discuss the rules:
   a. During the game, each person will receive the same amount of money. (If the class is too big, have the bidding done in teams of four or five)
   b. When there is an item that the students want, they are allowed to bid on it.
   c. If the students run out of money, they can no longer bid.
4. During the game, they are to write down the bidding values for each item auctioned off. This will be used in a classroom discussion following the game.
5. Following the activity, use the following discussion questions:
   a. Which tags went for the most amount of money?
   b. Which tags went for the least amount of money?
   c. Why do you think certain items were identified as more important than others?
   d. Which of these items do you see as a long-term value? Which item do you see as something that will be exciting "in the moment" but will mean less afterward?
6. Explain to the students that many times people highly value an item, then after they have it for a while, it is no longer that exciting to have.
   a. What are some things in life that never lose value?
   b. How might someone's desires and wants affect their behavior?
7. After discussion, distribute the Priority Assessment.

Data

Quantitative: 90% of the students will be able to identify the difference between a constant and a short-term want.

Answers for the Priority Assessment:

1. B
2. C
3. E
4. C
5. A

Total points for assessment: 5

Optional Lesson Extensions

(adding five to ten minutes to a lesson)

1. **The Stuff Life, The Good Life:** Have one group of students describe what it would be like to have a "Stuff Life." They are to create a list of objects, needs, and wants that could be categorized as "stuff." The other group of students will write paragraphs on what it would mean to have a "Good Life." They are to create a list of items that they would consider essential to have a good life. Discuss the various viewpoints, misconceptions, and points of similarity.
2. **Value-Pack:** On a large sheet of paper, have the class come up with a list of values that they think are long-term. With each item on the list, they must also explain why they view it as long-term.

Name: ______________________________ Date: ________________

Priority Assessment

1. **In the list below, which items may be important no matter how old you are?**
   a. A remote controlled car
   b. Good study skills
   c. A mp3 player
   d. A designer pair of jeans
   e. All of the above

2. **How can you tell if a want or need is going to be long-term or short-term?**
   a. If the want or need is popular with everyone else, it must be constant
   b. If the want or need is expensive, then it must be constant
   c. If the want or need is helpful and useful, then it must be constant
   d. If the want or need is really fun to use, then it must be constant
   e. All of the above

3. **What kinds of things will PROBABLY change as you grow older?**
   a. The games that you like to play with all the time
   b. Your favorite television shows
   c. The movies that you like to go see
   d. The way that you spend your free time
   e. All of the above

4. **A fifth grade girl is looking at a new camera phone that is very expensive. Which question can she ask to see if this is a long-term want or a short-term want?**
   a. Does this come in my favorite color?
   b. Will other people realize how cool this phone is?
   c. Will I like having this phone two years from now?
   d. How many text messages can I send on it?
   e. All of the above

5. **Which statement is TRUE about priorities?**
   a. There is a difference between what is popular and what is helpful and useful
   b. Once something is cool, it will be cool forever
   c. If I want it now, I will always want it
   d. It does not matter how I am treated, as along as I have lots of friends
   e. All of the above

Bidding Sheets

Directions: Use the bidding sheets to show how much items have sold for and which items you have won.

Bidding Sheet	How much did you pay for it?	How much did it sell for?
People caring about me		
Fame on television or in music		
Tickets to the NBA Finals		
Good decision making		
Family peace		
A good friend		
Honesty		
Popularity		
Kindness		
Good grades		
Finding a little happiness in everything		
A new mp3 player		
Athletic ability		
Resolving conflicts peacefully		

Bidding Tags

People caring about me
Fame on television or in music
Tickets to the NBA Finals
Good decision making
Family peace
A good friend
Honesty
Popularity
Good grades
Finding a little happiness in everything
A new mp3 player
Athletic ability
Resolving conflicts peacefully

Earnest Empathy

Overview

Students will learn how to give empathetic statements. They will practice communication skills that are appropriate to help students who are upset.

ASCA Standards

- PS.A2.6: Use effective communications skills
- PS.A2.7: Know that communication involves speaking, listening and nonverbal behavior
- PS.B1.4: Develop effective coping skills for dealing with problems

Materials

Empathy Assessment
Conversation Cards
Empathy Hint Card

Approximate Time: 30 minutes

Procedures

1. Explain to the students that today they are going to learn about how to give caring statements in very helpful ways. When students can give caring statements to other students, it helps build relationships and can make someone who is feeling bad feel a lot better! Empathy is when people understand how another person feels. Being empathetic to an upset person can help them feel better!
2. There are certain times when people think they are trying to help, but they are actually making someone feel worse!

Event that happened	Your classmate says
Student is sad because they failed a test.	Classmate says, "Why don't you just answer all the questions right?"
A student is crying because their favorite pet ran away.	Classmate says, "You'll get another pet, don't worry!"
A student's parents are getting a divorce.	Classmate says, "I bet you are going to have to find a new dad."

3. How would you feel if something sad happened to you and your classmate said something like the above examples? Does it seem like the classmate is giving a caring statement?
4. Some kids are trying to help by cheering up their classmates. Some kids don't know what to say if their friends are really sad. Explain that students can make a difference by giving a positive, caring statement. They just need to know how!
5. Students will learn three helpful hints for caring statements:
   a. **Identify** how the classmate feels. *(It looks like you are feeling sad)*
   b. **Repeat** the concern with a question or a statement. *(Are you upset because you failed a test? Failing the test seems to make you upset)*
   c. **Personalize** how it would make you feel if it happened to you. *(It would make me feel sad, too)*
6. Explain to the students that when their friends are upset, it can be helpful to communicate with them that you have an understanding of how they feel.
7. Have the class work through an example by using the Identify, Repeat, Personalize communication method. As an example:

Event: Your classmate was laughed at because she spilled fruit punch all over her shirt. The classmate begins to cry.

Identify statement: "It looks like you are feeling sad."

Repeat statement: "It can be upsetting when people laugh because of a silly accident."

Personalize statement: "I wouldn't like it either if people were laughing at me."

8. Distribute the Conversation Cards to the students. In pairs they are to go through and practice using the Identify, Repeat, Personalize method for caring communication. To further help, give each student an Empathy Hint Card.
9. When the students have finished going through the cards, ask the following discussion questions:
   a. How does giving a caring statement help someone who is upset? Potential answers:
      - The upset person understands that someone cares about them.

- The upset person feels like they are understood.

b. What does it mean to be empathetic? Potential answers:
- Trying to understand how someone feels.
- Showing someone that you can see why someone feels sad or upset.

c. What might happen if a student was really sad and you said to him, "Don't worry about it! Just cheer up!" Potential answers:
- The sad student might think you don't know how sad he/she is.
- The sad student might get more upset since he/she feels like no one cares.

10. Conclude by indicating that being empathetic does not mean trying to solve the other student's problem! Instead of helping a student "get over it," empathy lets the person know that they are cared for and that their feelings are important.

11. Distribute the Empathy Assessment.

Data

Qualitative: 90% of the students will be able to recognize empathetic statements. They will be able to identify how empathy can help students cope with problems.

Answers to the Empathy Assessment:

1. D
2. C
3. C
4. A
5. D

Total points for assessment: 5

Optional Lesson Extension

(adding five to ten minutes to a lesson)

1. **Personal**—After using the conversation cards, have students express times in their life they wish that someone was empathetic toward them or a time when they showed empathy.
2. **List it**—Students can write down a list of people they have not been empathetic toward. In the following week, they are to go and interact with the other person and show empathy.

Name: ____________________ **Date:** __________

Name: ______________________ Date: ______________

Empathy Assessment

1. **What is empathy?**
   - a. Making fun of someone for how they feel
   - b. Making a list of ways to cheer up their friend
   - c. Finding a solution to a problem
   - d. Understanding how someone else feels
   - e. None of the above

2. **Which of the following is an IDENTIFY statement:**
   - a. "That would make me feel sad, too"
   - b. "I wouldn't like it if someone pushed me around, either"
   - c. "It seems like you are really angry"
   - d. "What is the problem"
   - e. None of the above

3. **A classmate is angry because she did not make the all-star soccer team. Which of the following is an empathetic statement?**
   - a. "You should try out for the team next year"
   - b. "People get cut all the time from that team. The coach is mean"
   - c. "I feel angry too when I want something and I don't get it"
   - d. "I wouldn't feel too bad about it, I mess up all the time"
   - e. None of the above

4. **Which of the following is NOT part of using empathy?**
   - a. Problem-Solve
   - b. Identify
   - c. Repeat
   - d. Personalize
   - e. None of the above

5. **When is a good time to be empathetic to a classmate?**
   - a. If a classmate is upset over their grades
   - b. If a classmate is angry over losing a game
   - c. If a classmate is sad because of something that happened at home
   - d. All of the above
   - e. None of the above

Conversation Cards

Directions: Copy, cut, and distribute to the students. While working in pairs, one student read the conversation card and the other student will use the Identify, Repeat, Personalize communication method to practice empathy.

"When we moved to this new school, I had to leave all my friends behind."	**"I can't stand it when my teacher does not call on me when I know the answer. I think she does it on purpose!"**
"I'm really upset because my mom lost her job at the factory and I don't know what is going to happen."	**"I worked really hard on this project and I got a "D" on it! I am really frustrated!"**
"My best friend and I got into a fight and now we aren't best friends any more."	**"I wanted the class to vote for me for class president and I lost the election."**

Empathy Hint Card

Directions: Distribute these cards to the students as a reminder for the Identify, Repeat, and Personalize communication method.

Identify: Tell the person that you see how they are feeling!	**Identify:** Tell the person that you see how they are feeling!
Repeat: Make sure you understand why they are upset!	**Repeat:** Make sure you understand why they are upset!
Personalize: Let them know how you would feel if it happened to you!	**Personalize:** Let them know how you would feel if it happened to you!
Identify: Tell the person that you see how they are feeling!	**Identify:** Tell the person that you see how they are feeling!
Repeat: Make sure you understand why they are upset!	**Repeat:** Make sure you understand why they are upset!
Personalize: Let them know how you would feel if it happened to you!	**Personalize:** Let them know how you would feel if it happened to you!

Teeter-Talking

Overview

Students will learn how to participate in an appropriate conversation. They will learn how to engage another student in conversation and how to refrain from dominating the dialogue.

ASCA Standards

- PS.A1.8: Understand the need for self-control and how to practice it
- PS.A2.6: Use effective communications skills
- PS.A2.8: Learn how to make and keep friends

Materials

Communication Assessment
Conversation Cards
Chairs

Approximate Time: 30 minutes

Procedures

1. Ask the students to describe what it feels like to have a conversation where one person is talking all the time and the other person cannot say anything. Students may indicate:
   a. It is frustrating because the other person is the only one talking.
   b. It appears that the other person is not interested in what I have to say.
   c. It makes me mad because it is a one-sided conversation.
2. Explain that sometimes students do not realize they are having a one-sided conversation. Some students may want to say something, but the other person keeps going on and on!
3. Indicate to the students that a one-sided conversation is like a teeter-totter (or a see-saw) where one person is in the air the whole time and the other person is on the ground!
   a. Explain that the person in the air is the one who is doing all the talking.

b. Explain that the person on the ground is the one who is doing all the listening.

4. Ask, "If you were on a teeter-totter, would you want to be the person who is stuck on the ground?" Probably not because you are not getting to have as much fun as the person in the air!

5. Indicate that when one person "hogs" a conversation, the other person doesn't participate and can feel left out or unappreciated. They are just there to "hoist" the other person "up."

6. Explain to the students that they are going to practice "Teeter-Talking!"
   a. Two students will sit in chairs about a foot apart from each other. They will then practice a conversation. The student who is talking will stand up while the other student is sitting.
   b. When the standing student is finished speaking, he or she will sit and the sitting student will stand and begin their part of the conversation.

7. Just like when people use a teeter-totter, both people have to work together to make a conversation successful. There are two simple techniques that can help a conversation flow nicely.
   a. **Lift-Off Question:** A Lift-Off Question is when the talking student asks the other student to give their thoughts and ideas about the conversation. Some examples of a Lift-Off Question:
      - "What are your thoughts about that?"
      - "How do you feel about [whatever the topic is]?"
   b. **Prompting Push:** A Prompting Push is when one student prompts the conversation through picking a topic or asking the other student to create a new conversation subject. Some examples of a Prompting Push:
      - "Tell me about your favorite school subject."
      - "Is there something you want to talk about?"

8. Students that include each other through questions and prompts can help create friendships. They can learn more about each other.

9. Have one student come to the front of the class and demonstrate a successful conversation via "Teeter-Talking."

10. After the example, ask the following questions:
    a. What did you notice about the conversation? Potential answers:
       - You and the student were taking turns.
       - No one was hogging the conversation.
    b. How do you think it feels to know that the other person is interested in what you have to say? Potential answers:
       - It feels good to be appreciated.
       - It can help create friendships.

11. Place the students in pairs. The partners are to practice "Teeter-Talking." Give each student one or two of the conversation cards so they will have a topic to discuss.

12. After the students have concluded the activity, ask the following discussion questions:
    a. How do you think sharing a conversation can help you with friendships? Potential answers:
        - People who are friends work together and can share ideas.
        - Sharing a conversation can help people get to know someone else.
    b. How does sharing a conversation show self-control? Potential answers:
        - By sharing through prompts and questions, students can make sure they are not hogging a conversation.
        - It takes self-control to watch how much talking one student is doing.
13. Conclude the lesson by distributing the Communication Assessment.

Data

Quantitative: 90% of the students will be able to identify effective conversation skills. They will be able to demonstrate how to apply questions and prompts to create a balanced conversation with their peers.

Answers for Communication Assessment:

1. C
2. A
3. D
4. D
5. B

Total points for assessment: 5

Optional Lesson Extension

(adding five to ten minutes to a lesson)

1. **One-sided Conversation**—When the one student helps demonstrate how to use the "Teeter-Talking" techniques, show the students what it looks like to have a one sided conversation where one person stands the whole time while the other person just sits.
2. **List-O-Prompts**—Have the class develop a list of prompts that they can ask each other as a way to get an equally balanced conversation going. Some examples:
    a. Tell me about your brothers and sisters.
    b. Tell me about your favorite place.
    c. Tell me about the scariest thing that ever happened to you.

Name: ______________________ Date: __________

Communication Assessment

1. **How can you have a balanced and fair conversation?**
   a. Only talk about what you want to talk about
   b. Ask so many questions that you don't have to talk
   c. Talk for a little bit, then ask a question to let the other person talk
   d. Just stare at each other until one person decides to talk
   e. None of the above

2. **What can you do in a conversation to learn about another person?**
   a. Ask them about their favorite subjects
   b. Ask them to go get you your favorite type of ice cream
   c. Talk about yourself so they know that you are cool
   d. Ask the other person to agree with your ideas
   e. None of the above

3. **Why is it important to share a conversation?**
   a. It shows that you are interested in the other person
   b. It shows that you have self-control
   c. It shows the other person that you care about them
   d. All of the above
   e. None of the above

4. **What is a one-sided conversation?**
   a. Both students are talking and sharing ideas
   b. Both students are yelling to prove their point
   c. One student answers someone else's question
   d. One student talks the whole time
   e. None of the above

5. **Which statement is a good conversation prompt to give to a student you are talking to?**
   a. "Let me tell you all about me"
   b. "What do you think about our science project"
   c. "I got all of the answers right on our last test. Isn't that great"
   d. "Why don't we talk about how cool I am"
   e. None of the above

Conversation Cards

Directions: Cut and distribute to the pairs of students to practice a balanced, shared conversation.

Talk about the funniest thing that ever happened to you.

Talk about a time that you laughed so hard that you almost cried.

Talk about a time that you got in trouble.

Talk about a time that you were really sad.

Talk about a time when you thought you made the teacher mad.

Talk about a time when you got exactly what you wanted.

Talk about a time you were scared.

Talk about a time you did something really good.

Talk about a time you won something.

Talk about a time you lost a game.

Talk about your favorite movies.

Talk about your favorite game.

Talk about your least favorite dessert.

Talk about your least favorite subject.

Section Three:

Career Domain

Bank on It!

Overview

Students will learn that teamwork can divide a large task into small components, thus making it easier. Students will learn that effective communication is a key to successful teamwork.

ASCA Standards

- CD.C2.3: Learn how to work cooperatively with others as a team member
- PS.A2.6: *Use effective communication skills*

Materials:

Play money of various denominations
Bank Registry
Teamwork Assessment

Approximate Time: 30 Minutes

Procedures

1. Split the class up into groups of three or four.
2. Ask the students if they can think of anything that involves teamwork—appropriate answers may vary from sports teams to activities in school. Ask the students to consider a game of baseball:
   a. What would happen if you were on a baseball team and there was no catcher?
   b. What would it be like if there was no one playing first base?
3. Indicate to the students that teams are comprised of people who play different, but, very important roles. Say to the students, "Sure, you could play a game of baseball without a catcher, but it would be more difficult. And you could even play without a first baseman, but think of what other players would have to do to play the game!"
   a. Ask the students, "Can you think of other places where people have different roles to play to get a job done?"

   b. If students are having a difficult time, prompt them to think about the different jobs in constructing a house or when people are in a doctor's office—what role does the nurse play? What role does the receptionist play? What role does the doctor play?

4. Explain to the students that they are going to play a game where each group will be responsible for running a bank. Each person in the group will have a role at the bank:
   a. **The teller**—his or her job is to give and take money to/from the customer.
   b. **The accountant**—his or her job is to write down all the deposits and withdrawals on the bank registry.
   c. **The safe keeper**—he or she must keep the money organized; they receive the money from the teller and give the money to the teller.
   d. **The loan officer**—his or her job is to double check the work of the other three workers; to see if they are responsible for paying fines and receiving bank awards.
5. Before you play:
   a. Ask the students to name some of the keys to a successful teamwork experience, if they need help, prompt them with:
      - Communication, sharing, giving compliments, staying calm, using appropriate voices, good attitudes and positive support
6. How to Play:
   a. The teacher or the counselor will start each bank off with the same amount of money; they will then go from bank to bank at random and either deposit money or withdraw money as they see fit.
   b. Every few minutes, "audit" the bank. Ask the loan officer to count up the money in the bank—then check it against the bank registry. If the number is the same, then award them with a bonus deposit. If the money amount is different, then fine them with a hefty withdrawal.
      - If the bank does not have the correct amount of money, the bank is "closed" until the members can find out where they made their mistake; they must then correct the error before the bank can "open" again.
   c. At the end of the session, see which banks made the most money, which banks were closed down the least, and which banks had the most amount of trouble.
7. Discussion Questions:
   a. What behaviors made a bank successful? What behaviors made a bank struggle?
   b. If you are working with someone who makes a mistake, how can you address it?
   c. Why does "how you say things" matter sometimes as much as "what you say?"
   d. What do you think helps teams have success? What could you do to have more success?
8. Distribute the Teamwork Assessment.

Data

Quantitative: 90% of the students will be able to successfully identify the importance of teamwork and ways to work cooperatively.

Answers for the Teamwork Assessment:

1. D
2. A
3. A
4. E
5. C

Total points for assessment: 5

Optional Lesson Extensions

(adding five to ten minutes to a lesson)

1. **Silence**—During five minutes of the game, allow no talking.
   a. Did this make the game more difficult, why?
   b. What did you have to do to communicate?
   c. How did it feel to not be able to communicate like you normally do?
2. **Trickery**—If students are communicating well, make things more difficult by offering one amount of money, but saying a different amount: "I'd like to deposit ten dollars, please" but hand a five dollar bill to the teller.
3. **Role Play**—Before the Bank Game begins, role play with the teacher and two other students a team that is showing the worst kind of teamwork—make this as humorous as possible!!!

Name: ______________________ **Date:** ______________

Teamwork Assessment

1. **What is good about teamwork?**
   a. Projects get done quicker because everyone is doing one part at a time
   b. People divide up the work so classmates who don't get along can be left alone
   c. An assignment becomes easier to do because everyone can copy off of each other's answers
   d. People split up the work so each person has a little bit to do and more can get accomplished
   e. All of the above

2. **Why is communication important for teamwork?**
   a. So everyone knows what they need to do to help and how they are doing
   b. So everyone knows who is the boss and who is the follower
   c. So everyone understands that if one person makes a mistake, the whole project will be ruined
   d. So everyone understands who the best worker is and who the worst worker is
   e. All of the above

3. **Which statement would be more likely to help a team out?**
   a. "If you need help, I can help show you how to do some of it"
   b. "You are doing it all wrong! Just let me do it"
   c. "That's not my job; you have to figure it out"
   d. "Why do I always have to do everyone else's job"
   e. All of the above

4. **How can you be a good team member?**
   a. Give positive support
   b. If someone is confused, explain politely what he or she needs to do
   c. Talk out differences instead of arguing
   d. Treat everyone in the group with respect
   e. All of the above

5. **When will you need to use teamwork?**
   a. When you are reading a book
   b. While you are taking a test
   c. When your family has a bunch of chores to do at home
   d. When your teacher asks you to deliver a note
   e. All of the above

Name: ______________________ Date: ______________

Bank Registry

Directions: Keep track of your money! Write down the amount of money you have. Circle whether the teacher and counselor have given a withdrawal or deposit. Write down how much money you have left in the bank! If the amount of cash is different from what is on your registry, your bank will be closed!

Money Amount	Is it a withdrawal or a deposit?		Starting Amount:
	Withdrawal -	Deposit +	Current Amount of Money in the Bank
	Withdrawal -	Deposit +	
	Withdrawal -	Deposit +	
	Withdrawal -	Deposit +	
	Withdrawal -	Deposit +	
	Withdrawal -	Deposit +	
	Withdrawal -	Deposit +	
	Withdrawal -	Deposit +	
	Withdrawal -	Deposit +	
	Withdrawal -	Deposit +	

How many times did you get audited? ______________________

How many times did your bank close? ______________________

Who is Your Role Model?

Overview

Students will recognize how to identify whether someone is a good candidate as a role model; students will identify characteristics of role models that they admire.

ASCA Standards

- CD.A1.3: Develop an awareness of personal abilities, skills, interests, and motivations.
- CD.A1.8: Pursue and develop competency in areas of interest.

Materials

Role Model Characteristic Form
Identifying Role Models Assessment

Approximate Time: 30 minutes

Procedures

1. Ask the students, "When you think of a role model, who comes to mind?" Students may identify:
   a. Teachers
   b. Members of the Community
   c. Parents
   d. Famous individuals (actors, musicians, athletes)
   e. Fictional Characters
2. Identify role models as people who have characteristics that we might like to have. Ask the students what characteristics they want to have.
   a. Smart, wealthy, funny, strong, fast, kind, witty, etc.
3. Ask the students, "If someone is famous or wealthy, does that mean they are worth looking up to as a role model?"

   a. Indicate, we may think that someone is a good role model because they are on television or because we know that they have "become successful" for whatever reason, but that does not necessarily mean that we know whether or not they have the characteristics we hope to have one day.
      - Being wealthy or famous does not necessarily make a person a good role model—it is what kind of person they are, not the job they perform.

4. Lead the students into a discussion based on two topics: What kind of person are you motivated to become and what questions could you ask someone to see if they are a good role model?
5. Distribute the Role Model Characteristic Form:
   a. The students are to check off the characteristics that they would like to aspire to have.
   b. Next, the students are to think of someone who fits those characteristics.
   c. Finally, the students are to write down "interview questions" that could allow them to see whether or not the person fits their schema. Some examples:
      - What do you think is the most important part of your day and why?
      - What goals did you have as a kid? How did you accomplish them?
      - What do you value as a grown-up? What did you value as a kid?
6. Have the students share their role models and their role model interview questions.
7. Conclude the lesson by distributing the Identifying Role Models Assessment.

Data

Quantitative: 90% of the students will be able to identify what a role model is, questions to ask a role model, and the difference between being a good role model and being a recognized individual.

Student-Centric: Through the students Role Model Characteristic Form, record what the classroom recognizes as the most important characteristics that they wish they could have when they get older. Also the form will show whom the classroom identifies as role models.

Answers to the Identifying Role Models Assessment:

1. C
2. C
3. B
4. E
5. C

Total points for assessment: 5

Optional Lesson Extensions

(adding five to ten minutes to a lesson)

1. **In the news**—Have students look through newspapers and identify people who may be good role models and people who are well-known. Indicate that role models can be well-known people, but that does not always hold true. Have the students write the admirable characteristics of the role models by their pictures.
2. **Contact your role model**—Once the students pick a person (or people) who they think are worthy role models, have them try to contact that person through e-mail or writing a letter and asking the interview questions.

Name: ______________________ **Date:** ______________

Identifying Role Models Assessment

1. **What is a role model?**
   a. A person who is on my favorite television show
   b. A person who has characteristics that I don't like
   c. A person who has qualities that I hope to have one day
   d. A person who is pretty, rich, and has lots of friends
   e. None of the above
2. **What "interview question" would be helpful in identifying a role model?**
   a. What is it like to have lots of money?
   b. Do you think that you have the best job in the world?
   c. What did you have to do to reach your goals?
   d. Can I have your autograph?
   e. None of the above
3. **True or False: People who are professional athletes, movie stars, or music stars are all worthy role models?**
   a. True
   b. False
4. **How can having a role model be helpful?**
   a. You can see someone who sets a good example
   b. You can learn what that person did to become successful
   c. You can see what you will have to do to reach your goals
   d. You can find ways that you are similar to a successful person
   e. None of the above
5. **Which of the following DOES NOT have to do with a role model's character?**
   a. Humble
   b. Kind
   c. Wealthy
   d. Sincere
   e. None of the above

Name: ______________________ **Date:** ______________

Role Model Characteristic Form

What kind of characteristics are you motivated to have? Pick your top FOUR.

	Smart: a person who thinks and solves problems
	Respectful: a person who treats all people the same
	Kind: a person who is nice to others
	Humble: someone who does not show off
	Strong: this person has big muscles
	Athletic: someone who is good at sports
	Honest: someone who tells the truth…no matter what
	Funny: a person who makes people laugh
	Clean: a person who keeps their things neat and in order
	Loud: a person who has a voice that is heard easily by everyone
	Attractive: a person who people think is handsome or pretty
	Quiet: a person who speaks softly
	Shy: a person who makes a few friends and does not have to get all of the attention
	Serious: a person who is very focused and does not joke around too much
	Happy: someone who is in a good mood a lot
	Rich: someone who has a lot of money

Who do you think would match the characteristics that you hope to have one day? Name the person you think would be a good role model: ______________________

What are three interview questions that you would want to ask to find out if the person might be a good role model?

1.

2.

3.

Do the Math!

Overview

Students will be able to identify how to set a goal.

ASCA Standards

- CD.A1.6: Learn how to set goals
- CD.A1.7: Understand the importance of planning
- PS.B1.12: *Develop an action plan to set and achieve realistic goals*

Materials

Goal Setting Reproducible
Planning and Goal Setting Assessment

Approximate Time: 30 Minutes

Procedures

1. Ask the students to describe several things that they want: their wants can be anything from a new game system to good grades.
2. Explain to the students that most of the time, when we want something, we don't just get it when we ask. Ask, "If you wanted to make straight "A"s, would your teacher just give them to you? If you wanted to be the best soccer player in the school, would that happen by doing nothing?"
3. By setting out a plan, people are more likely to achieve their goals—ask, "If you wanted to pass a history test, what are some steps that you would have to take to reach it?"
   a. Students may say study, pay attention, work hard.
4. Explain, reaching your goals is a little bit like math:
   a. When you are making plans, it is important to think of what you can do to help you get what you want:

- Part 1 + Part 2 = Goal
- If you want to get an A on a spelling test, it may look like this:
  1. Make and use flash cards + write a song with the words = Get an A
  2. Study the words every night + use the words in a story = Get an A

5. On the board, have the students think of some examples of steps that it will take to reach a goal.
   a. For a new bike: Mow the neighbors lawn + save birthday money = a new bike
   b. A good behavior report: listen to the teacher + follow rules = good behavior report
6. Have the students also think of some things that "don't add up."
   a. Go to the circus + stay up way too late = finish every bit of homework
   b. Throw food at lunch + talk in the hallway = extra privileges
7. Distribute the Goal Setting Reproducible.
   a. When the students are done setting their three goals, have people share—see if the class believes that the expectations and goals are realistic.
   b. Indicate for the students to write down who needs to see the plan—some of their goals may need approval by parents. Some goals may need more than two parts to it!
8. Conclude by letting the students know that planning for goals is a mature and productive way to getting a want. Rather than just hoping someone helps them get what they want, students can get close to their goals by taking action!
9. Distribute the Planning and Goal Setting Assessment.

Data

Quantitative: 90% of the students will be able to recognize the importance of creating plans to reach their goals.

Student-Centric: Follow up with students using their Goal Setting Reproducible to see who successfully accomplished a goal (or goals) from the form.

Answers for the Planning and Goal Setting Assessment:

1. C
2. C,E (two points)
3. A
4. D
5. C

Totally points for the assessment: 5

Optional Lesson Extensions

(adding five to ten minutes to a lesson)

Building Blocks: Split the students into groups and have the students draw blueprints for a building. The groups will then send their blueprints to another table for that group to build the design.

Discussion Questions: Did the building turn out the way you thought it would? If not, how could you have changed your plans to make it easier to accomplish? If it did, how does making clear plans help you reach your goal?

Name: ______________________ Date: ____________

Planning and Goal Setting Assessment

1. **What is the best way to get what you want?**
   a. Ask until my parents or teacher give in
   b. Stay quiet until someone realizes what I want
   c. Make a plan and see if my parent/teacher agrees
   d. Throw a temper tantrum until I get what I want
   e. None of the above

2. **If you wanted to pass a spelling test, what would your *TWO PARTS* of the plan be? Circle *two* of the answers below:**
   a. Reading books that are easy to read
   b. Looking at the words for the first time right before the test
   c. Writing the words and using them in sentences all week
   d. Watching T.V. and hoping you hear the words on your favorite show
   e. Play a spelling game with a friend to help study

3. **Why is it important to create a plan?**
   a. To know what needs to be accomplished to reach a goal
   b. To make sure you don't keep asking your parents for what you want
   c. To know how to stay busy so you don't think about the goal
   d. To make sure that people see you working hard
   e. None of the above

4. **You want to get a black belt in Karate—which plans would you choose?**
   a. Teach friends karate moves + make a list of skills needed for a black belt
   b. Read books on karate + practice kicks in the evening
   c. Have good attendance to karate class + ask the instructor questions
   d. All are good plans to get a black belt in Karate
   e. None of the above

5. **What happens if your plans to get you to your goal do not work?**
   a. Realize that you need a new goal
   b. Consider the goal too hard to reach
   c. Realize that you need to think of a new set of plans
   d. Consider trying the same plans again and again

Name: ______________________________ **Date:** ______________

Goal Setting Reproducible

Decide on a goal you want and write down who needs to approve your goal. Then write down the steps that add together to reach your goal!

What is my goal? ______________________________

Who needs to approve my goal? ______________________________

Part 1		Part 2		Goal
	+		=	

What is my goal? ______________________________

Who needs to approve my goal? ______________________________

Part 1		Part 2		Goal
	+		=	

What is my goal? ______________________________

Who needs to approve my goal? ______________________________

Part 1		Part 2		Goal
	+		=	

The Domino Effect

Overview

Students will learn that the decisions they make may directly impact their consequences.

ASCA Standards

- CD.A1.4: Learn how to make decisions
- CD.A1.7: Understand the importance of planning
- PS.A1.6: *Distinguish between appropriate and inappropriate behavior*
- PS.B1.2: *Understand consequences of decisions and choices*

Materials

Dominos (or any type of material that can be set up for a "chain reaction")
Domino Effect Form
Decision and Consequence Assessment

Approximate Time: 30 Minutes

Procedures

1. Explain to the students that making decisions and receiving consequences are very similar to cause and effect. When we make a decision, that is just like a cause—and when we receive a consequence, that is just like an effect.
   a. Ask the students to think of some other cause-and-effect relationships. If students don't know, indicate:
      - Eating a lot of food and becoming stuffed
      - Running a lot and getting tired
2. In the front of the class, set up a line of dominos. Pick up the first domino and ask, "How is this domino, the one at the front of the line, like a decision?"
   a. After taking appropriate answers, state, "When one decision is made, there are a chain of events that occur that are called *consequences*."

b. Give the first domino a decision and then follow the chain of consequences. For example:
   - This first domino represents a student who stayed up too late watching a movie...
   - Which made him late for school...
   - Which caused him to miss his breakfast...
   - Which made him hungry...
   - Which made it very difficult to concentrate...
   - Which caused him to miss some very easy questions on a quiz he had to take.

c. Push the dominos down, ask, "How can one decision affect the whole day?"

3. Distribute the Domino Effect Form to each student.
   a. Each student will use the form to tell different stories of a decision that was made.
   b. They can choose to make a story where an appropriate or inappropriate decision was made.
   c. Afterward, have the students share their Domino Stories. Some discussion questions:
      - What did you notice happening in the stories with appropriate decisions?
      - What did you notice about the stories with inappropriate decisions?
      - How can one decision affect the whole day?
      - If you see that you have made an inappropriate decision, what needs to happen to make the day better?
      - How can you tell which decisions will be appropriate and which ones will be inappropriate?
   d. Say, "When you are about to make a decision, think about the domino effect that will occur once your decision is made. When you consider what the consequences are before you make your decision, you will have a much better chance of making an appropriate choice."

4. Distribute the Decision and Consequence Assessment.

Data

Quantitative: 90% of the students will be able to identify how consequences are related to their decisions.

Answers for the Decision and Consequence Assessment:

1. B
2. A
3. B
4. D
5. C

Total points for assessment: 5

Optional Lesson Extensions

(adding five to ten minutes to a lesson)

1. **Multi-colored Dominos**—Where one color indicates a decision and another color indicates a consequence. While setting up the initial Domino Effect story, place the decision colored dominos into the line; this may indicate that even though an initial decision was made, other decisions can still affect the outcomes.
2. **Act It Out**—Have the students work in groups to act out a Domino Effect Story. Have each group tell the story in two different versions—one with inappropriate decisions and the other with appropriate decisions
3. **Additional Reading**—Read, *If You Give a Mouse a Cookie* by Laura Joffe Numeroff to discuss how chain of events occur.

Name: ______________________ Date: ____________

Decision and Consequence Assessment

1. **Phillip works all week on a project and gets an "A" on it. What was the decision?**
   a. He wanted to have fun and play all week
   b. He wanted to work all week on it to do a good job
   c. He wanted to do a little bit of work and then play with his friends
   d. He did not make any decision and got the "A" because he was lucky
   e. All of the above
2. **Jennifer works all day in her front yard cleaning up leaves. When she finishes, her father gives her ten dollars. What was the consequence of this event?**
   a. She earned ten dollars
   b. The girl works all day in the front yard
   c. The front yard has a bunch of leaves on the ground
   d. The girl jumped in the leaves
   e. All of the above
3. **When making a decision, when should you think about the result?**
   a. After the decision has been made
   b. Before the decision has been made
   c. You should never think about the result
   d. When your family tells you what to do
   e. All of the above
4. **Why is it important to think about the results of a decision?**
   a. Because some decisions may lead to bad results
   b. Because it can help you pick the best decision to make
   c. Because you can figure out what will be best for you
   d. All of the above
   e. None of the above
5. **Predict the most likely outcome: All day during school, Billy paid little attention to the teacher and goofed off during math.**
   a. Billy might get a prize from his teacher the next day
   b. Billy might make an "A+" on his math test
   c. Billy might get a call home to his family
   d. Billy might get ten dollars from his mom and dad for his behavior
   e. None of the above

Name: ______________________ **Date:** ______________

Domino Effect Form

Directions: Write your decision and the effects of the decision, then illustrate the decision and the consequence!

You have a test tomorrow, tell what happens!

Decision! →	→	→	Consequence!

Illustrate your DECISION	Illustrate your CONSEQUENCE

You have a lot of homework, tell what happens!

Decision! →	→	→	Consequence!

Illustrate your DECISION	Illustrate your CONSEQUENCE

Receive and You Shall Ask

Overview

Students will learn how to de-escalate bullying through the strategy of asking questions.

ASCA Standards

- CD.C2.2: Learn how to use conflict management skills with peers and adults
- PS.C1.10: *Learn techniques for managing stress and conflict*

Materials

Teaser Assessment
Teaser Cards

Approximate Time: 30 minutes

Procedures

1. Ask the students, "What are the least effective ways of dealing with someone who teases you?" Take appropriate responses before leading into the discussion of bully de-escalation methods.
2. Explain, "Today we are going to learn two effective ways of dealing with someone who teases or bullies: and both of them involve a special communication technique—talking!"
   a. The first technique is **Agreement**: with this technique, simply go along with what the person is saying, even if it is the furthest thing from the truth.
      - Someone might say, "Gosh, I know you are right. I never thought about it like that."
      - "Really, thanks for bringing that to my attention. You've been a big help today."
   b. The second technique is **Questioning**: with this technique, ask the teaser question after question.

- One might say, "What do you mean I don't do well? How would you know about that? Do you really like to know other people's business? How come?"
- "Did you think of that on your own? How did you get so creative? How long did it take for you to think of that?"

3. When people can engage the teaser through conversation, it begins to wear away a sense of power. What starts off as a way to hurt someone begins to turn into a conversation. This can be frustrating for the teaser or it can be distracting.
4. Ask for two volunteers to role play the two techniques with the following situation:
    a. Someone comes up to you and says that your clothes are not matching and way out of style.
5. Ask the students to get into pairs and distribute the Teaser Cards. They are to discuss which technique they would use if the Teaser Card really happened.
6. Have each dyad role-play to the class how they would handle the situation. Have one student read the card as the "teaser" and have the other student use the technique—when the role play is complete, ask the class to identify whether Agreement or Questioning was used.
7. Distribute the Teaser Assessment, collect the Teaser Cards.

Data

Quantitative: 90% of the students will be able to use Agreement or Questioning as a de-escalation technique to teasing.

Answers for the Teaser Assessment:

1. A
2. B
3. B
4. D

Total points for assessment: 6

Name: ______________________________ **Date:** ______________

Teaser Assessment

Pick the most appropriate response that uses Agreement or Questioning for the following statements:

1. **You are so awful at kick ball. Nobody likes a loser!**
   - **a.** "Does being awful at kickball make me a loser"
   - **b.** "I hate when you tease me"
   - **c.** "Be quiet! You are terrible at baseball"
   - **d.** "Oh yeah? How come you got an "F" on that test"
   - **e.** None of the above
2. **I can't imagine how you got to the 5th grade. Do you know anything?**
   - **a.** "You are so mean"
   - **b.** "Well, I am glad to be in the fifth grade"
   - **c.** "I can't believe you are in the fifth grade, too"
   - **d.** "I heard that you cheated to get in this grade. Is that true"
   - **e.** None of the above
3. **I heard when you go home, you watch baby cartoons and drink out of a bottle. You big baby!**
   - **a.** "You're the baby"
   - **b.** "How do you know my afternoon schedule"
   - **c.** "Why don't you drink a big bottle"
   - **d.** "I bet you cry when you go home"
   - **e.** None of the above
4. **You better get in the back of the lunch line. You are going to eat all the food!**
   - a. "Don't make fun of me"
   - **b.** "You should stop eating food, too"
   - **c.** "What's the point of talking to a jerk like you"
   - **d.** "Yes, I really am hungy"
   - **e.** None of the above

Teaser Cards

Directions: Distribute to students. They are to use Questioning and Agreement as bullying de-escalation techniques.

"Everybody passed the test but you; you must not be that smart."

"You eat more dessert than anyone in the class. You are going to be a whale!"

"You are such a shrimp! I bet you can't even pick up your book bag!"

"You are the funniest looking kid in our school. I bet you break mirrors that you look at."

"You can't sit at this table. This is only where the cool kids are going to sit and you definitely are not cool."

"You know that everybody in our class doesn't like you. They wish that you would move!"

"You need to go home and just stay there. No one wants to be your friend."

"Don't you need to go back to kindergarten? I bet you don't even know how to count to ten."

"You are the most annoying kid in the class; you are never going to never have any friends."

A Time Piece

Overview

Students will learn how to create a balanced schedule. They will recognize the importance of appropriate planning.

ASCA Standards

- CD.A1.7: Understand the importance of planning
- CD.A1.10: Balance between work and leisure time
- CD.A2.9: Utilize time- and task-management skills

Materials

Planning Assessment
Time Piece Reproducible
Marker Board and Markers

Approximate Time: 30 minutes

Procedures

1. Explain to the students that an important key to being successful at school is to have a good balance with all parts of the day. Students that are rested and relaxed will probably be more focused at school. Today's lesson will be about creating a balanced schedule.
2. On the board the students are going to give ideal use of time for a student's day. They will do this first by creating a list of day's activities. Some may use the following suggestions:
   a. School
   b. Clubs or Sports
   c. Time with friends
   d. Watching Television
   e. Doing homework

f. Eating meals
g. Chores

3. Create a pie chart with the students' suggestions. Guide the students to the most balanced day in between school, clubs, sports, and other activities. An example of a completed graph:

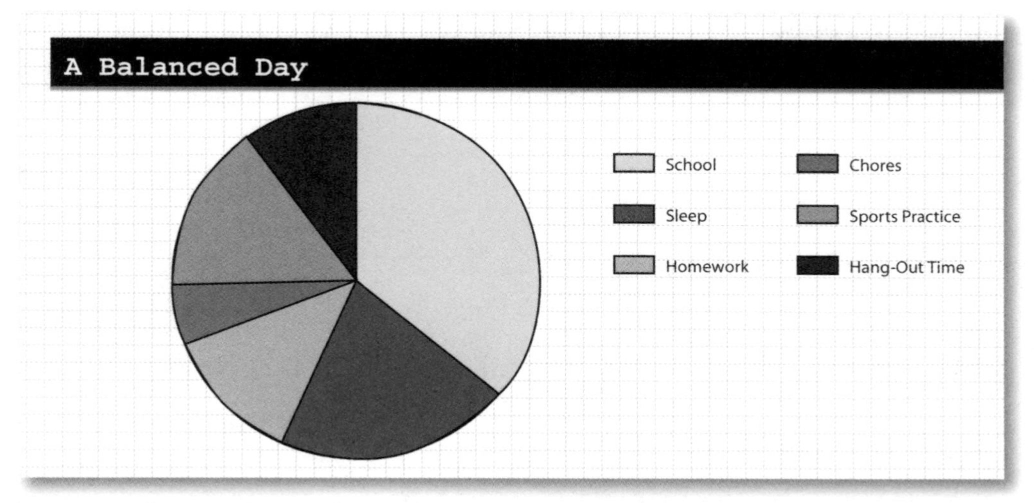

Note to the students that a balanced day does not mean that every activity is split up evenly. Some activities last longer than others. When a student is considering how to balance their day, here are some simple questions they can ask themselves:
a. How much time do I need to finish my work?
b. How much time do I need to relax and unwind?
c. How much sleep do I need to feel refreshed for the next day?

4. Next, distribute the Time Piece reproducible. The students are to come up with what they considered a balanced day for them. The students will use the activity list on their reproducible as a reference to events that occur during the day.
a. If students wish to supplement their own ideas, they can also write them in the activity list.

5. After their graphs are complete, students can share with the classmates or the whole class what they see as a balanced, ideal daily schedule.

6. Discussion questions to ask:
- What were the similarities between various students' schedules?
- Are there certain areas that you would be okay with changing?
- What would happen if you had a major project to do? What would change on your daily routine?
- How does writing out a daily schedule help you achieve a balanced day?
- How can free-time help with your school day? How much free-time is probably too much?

7. Conclude the lesson by distributing the Planning Assessment.

Data

Quantitative: 90% of the students will be able to recognize the importance of a balanced schedule. Students will be able to identify what a balanced schedule looks like and how to create a balanced schedule.

Answers to the Planning Assessment

1. C
2. D
3. B
4. A

Total points for assessment: 4

Optional Lesson Extension

(adding five to ten minutes to a lesson)

1. **More Planning**—Students can get even more specific by identifying which subjects need the most homework time. When students are doing their homework, which subject comes first? Which subject comes second?
2. **Estimation**—Students can create predictions of what a balanced daily schedule is for a working adult. While adults don't have to do homework, what activities take up most of their time? What can an adult in a career do to have a balanced day?

Name: ______________________ Date: ______________

Planning Assessment

1. **What is a balanced day?**
   a. A day where you are only doing one activity
   b. A day where you are moving from one activity to the next
   c. A day that is a mix of relaxing activities and school-work activities
   d. A day that is a mix of sleeping and napping and television watching
   e. None of the above
2. **What questions can help you create a balanced day?**
   a. How much time do I need to finish my work?
   b. How much time do I need to relax and unwind?
   c. How much sleep do I need to feel refreshed for the next day?
   d. All of the above
   e. None of the above
3. **A balanced day...**
   a. Means that every activity takes up the same amount of time
   b. Means that there is time for work and some time for fun
   c. Means that each day is very different and the schedule changes
   d. Means only doing the things I like to do
   e. None of the above
4. **What is the MOST helpful way of creating a balanced day?**
   a. Creating a chart of daily activities
   b. Drawing a picture favorite sports players
   c. Writing down a list of favorite television shows
   d. Writing down the books the teacher will make you read for the year
   e. None of the above

Name: ______________________________ **Date:** ________________

Time Piece Reproducible

Directions: Using the activity list, create what you think would be a balanced day. Which activities should take up a large part of the day? Which activities should take up a smaller part of the day? If you want to create your own Activity List, use the extra spaces.

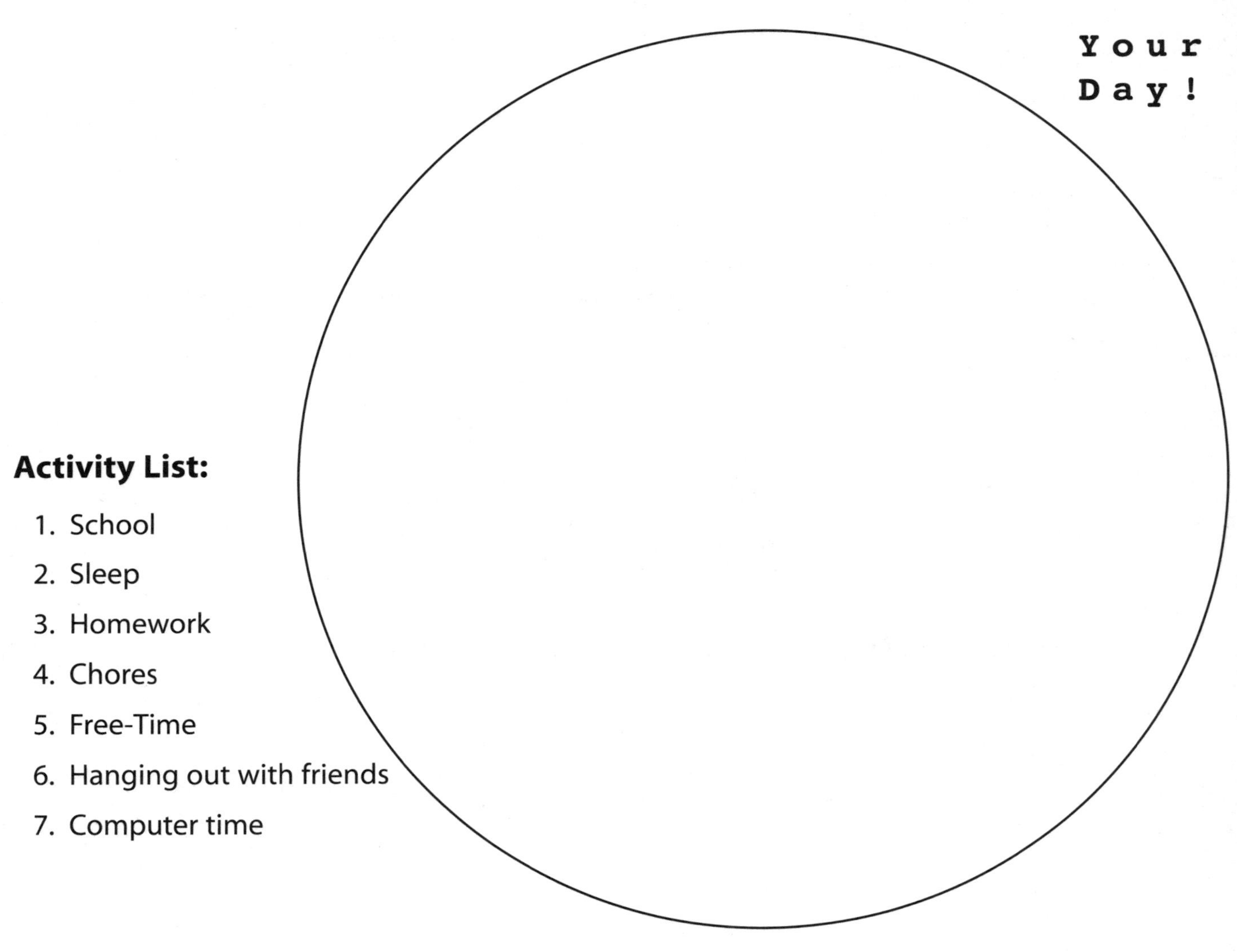

Your Day!

Activity List:

1. School
2. Sleep
3. Homework
4. Chores
5. Free-Time
6. Hanging out with friends
7. Computer time

Create your own!

1.	4.	7.
2.	5.	8.
3.	6.	9.

References

Curry, J. & Lambie, G. (2007). Enhancing school counselor accountability: The large group guidance portfolio. *Professional School Counseling*, 11, 145-148.

Dahir, C. & Stone, C. (2007). *School Counselor Accountability: A MEASURE of Student Success.* Columbus, OH: Pearson Merrill Prentice Hall.

Issacs, M. (2003). Data-Driven Decision Making: *The Engine of Accountability. Professional School Counseling*, 6, 288-295.

Nims, D., James, S., & Hughey, A. (1998). The challenge of accountability: A survey of Kentucky school counselors. *Kentucky Counseling Association*, 17, 31-37.

Whiston, S. C. (2002). Response to the past, present, and future of school counseling: Raising some issues. *Professional School Counseling*, 5, 148-155.

For more information on the American School Counselor Association domains, competencies, and standards, please visit:

www.schoolcounselor.org

Or write to:

American School Counselor Association
1101 King Street, Suite 625
Alexandria, VA 22314

About the Author

Anthony Pearson is the 2008-2009 Cobb School Counselor Association President, a member of the Counselor Advisory Team for the county, and has helped create the Cobb County Lesson Plan Website for School Counselors. He has been the After School Program Director and Den Master for the Boy Scouts Soccer and Scouting program.

Anthony graduated from Presbyterian College with a degree in Psychology before attending Auburn University to attain his Master's in School Counseling. He completed his Specialist in Education from Georgia State University.

In his spare time, he enjoys writing short stories, playing soccer, and finding good quotes from books.

Anthony lives in Atlanta, Georgia with his wife, Elizabeth, and their baby daughter, Ella.